The Man Who Changed China

The Story of Sun Yat-sen

THE MAN WHO

CHANGED CHINA

The Story of Sun Yat-sen

BY PEARL BUCK

Illustrated by FRED CASTELLON

RANDOM HOUSE · NEW YORK

Contents

1. Time for Change — 1
2. The Broken Gods — 19
3. The Revolutionist — 31
4. A Hunted Man — 51
5. A Troubled People — 64
6. The Waiting Time — 83
7. The Hunchback — 95
8. The Outbreak — 110
9. A Nation United — 123
10. Civil Wars — 142
11. "Save My Country" — 165
    Index — 183

1

Time for Change

THE VAST AND ANCIENT COUNTRY OF CHINA WAS
ready for change. The sleeping dragon, her neighbors called her, but the dragon was in trouble and
waking up.

What was China, nearly a hundred years ago?

The biggest country in the world except for
Russia, a third again as big as the United States,
the oldest country in the world, the most varied
country in the world—that was China. Five hun-

dred years before Christ was born Chinese wise men were already teaching people how to be good to one another, how to be industrious and civilized and strong. Artists were painting great works of art; architects were building handsome temples and palaces and houses; sculptors were carving fine statues; weavers were making beautiful brocades of satin and silk; farmers were tilling their fields until the land was in gardens; scholars were writing books and teaching in schools.

Long before America was discovered, other peoples all over Asia and indeed all over the known world, admired China and her noble civilization. So wonderful a civilization was it that no army or navy was needed. More than once foreign conquerors had captured the throne of government in Peking, but the Chinese had not needed to fight. They knew that in time, and even in a short time, their superior civilization would overcome the military conquerors. Time was always on the side of China. Everybody who came to live there always became Chinese.

What then was the trouble in China in that year of 1866? Outwardly the people were what they had always been. In the cities the streets were busy with men and women buying and selling; the shops were full and business was good. Farmers brought their vegetables, grains and fruits to great markets; fishermen showed their fish; and butchers hung their meats, scrubbed and clean, for everyone to see. Children laughed and played in the villages, and boys helped the men in the fields, and girls worked beside their mothers in the big lively farmstead homes. The feast days of New Year and the seasons were celebrated with all the old noise and laughter and good foods, and in the temples the gilded gods received the worshipers who came to give thanks and to pray.

Everything was the same and yet nothing was the same. Perhaps the children did not know of change, but the older people knew. The great spreading country was in trouble. A frightful rebellion had ended only two years earlier. It was the Taiping Rebellion, when many discontented and unhappy men had followed a half-mad leader who wanted to overthrow the Manchu government in Peking.

Why a Manchu government in the Chinese capital? Two hundred years earlier bold and ignorant men from Manchuria in the north had invaded China, and had seized the throne. In two hundred years they had become Chinese in many ways, but they had also become weak. They had grown rich and soft and had taken to enjoying themselves in the imperial gardens and palaces instead of caring for the welfare of the people. Now a weak emperor had married a bold and strong young wife. And when he died, she became the Empress Dowager. She was too ignorant to rule well, and the country was disturbed. Evil men rose up and were not checked. The rebellion, while it had been put down, had left many dead, and whole areas were burned and destroyed.

Earlier there had been three wars with England over the sale of opium in China, and the Chinese had lost all three wars. They had to pay large sums of money and, worst of all, to accept the opium which weakened the people who used it. Taxes were so high that people could not pay them. They were dissatisfied with the cruel government which took from them and gave nothing in return. Yes, it was time for a change.

"We must change our rulers," the people declared. "When the price of rice is too high for us to buy our food, Heaven decrees new rulers."

This was an old proverb, but the people believed it. Under their everyday life they were troubled and restless.

Time for a change! The whole world was changing, and they must change with it. England and

France and Germany and Spain and Portugal and at last even the United States were sending ships of war and ships of trade to China. The Chinese heard of railroads and steam engines, of gold mines in California and sugar plantations in Hawaii. Young men left home to go abroad, and they came back again to feel dissatisfied with the old village life and the quiet ancient cities. Even in the villages where the farm families lived, there was rising discontent.

In spite of all this, the Sun family in the village of Choyhung were happy in this year of 1866. A baby boy had been born to them when the father and mother were middle-aged. It was a lucky event. Father Sun was a farmer, and he thought it lucky because he could always do with another boy on the farm, especially since his older son, Ah-mei, did not like to farm. Mother Sun was proud of herself, for her last child had been a girl.

The new baby had black eyes and hair, a round

6

face, and smooth cream-colored skin. He was healthy, and when he cried he had a loud voice. But these two parents, living in a small Chinese village near the great city of Canton, in South China, and proud as they were, could not possibly know that this new baby son was no ordinary child. He was to become Sun Yat-sen, the man who changed China.

Father and Mother Sun themselves never thought about change. They lived in a pleasant farmhouse made of gray brick and thatched with straw, and they worked hard in the house and in the fields. The house was old, for their ancestors had lived in it before them, and as the years slipped away, they had expected that nothing would ever happen to them. Then came this surprising new baby. They were happy to have him, and as was the custom they gave their friends hard-boiled eggs, dyed red, for an announcement gift. When the baby was a month old, they invited all the

7

They had a feast when the baby was a month old

neighboring farmers to a feast. The baby, dressed
in a bright red suit, stared at everybody, smiled,
and looked like any other baby. But the farmers
congratulated the parents with special warmth. It
was luck, they said, to have a son when two people were no longer young.

It was not long before Father and Mother Sun
began to believe, too, that perhaps this son of

8

theirs was not a common farmer's child. He was very determined, he sat up early and he walked long before he was a year old. Mother Sun said, "We have the most mischievous boy in the village." Nothing could be put beyond his reach. He would always get it somehow. Never was such a boy for climbing high to get what he wanted. He was afraid of nobody and of nothing. He ran everywhere, and he followed the wandering jugglers and the men with performing monkeys.

"We must put him to school early," Father Sun said.

When he was still quite small, then, Yat-sen was sent to school. His mother dressed him in a long blue cotton robe and braided his hair tight with a red cord. In those days Chinese men and boys wore their hair in a braid. It was very much as men in Europe and America had once done, but the Chinese men let their hair grow longer. In China, however, men's braided hair was a sign of submission to the Manchu conquerors, those rough barbaric tribesmen who centuries before had come riding their shaggy ponies down from the north to conquer China.

School in the village began at seven o'clock and lasted until dark, and so before seven every morning Yat-sen trudged down the cobbled street to the schoolroom and sat down at his desk, which was a table with a stool. All the boys sat facing the teacher. There were little boys and big boys, and each one studied at his own pace, for there were no grades or classes. The teacher heard each pupil's lesson when it was learned. The lessons were to memorize some old books called *The Classics*. The first one, *The Three-Character Classic*, was the easiest and that was the one Yat-sen had now to begin.

As he memorized, he learned to read the characters, and he learned how to write by tracing those same characters on thin paper. When he had memorized his pages for the day, he had to take his book to the teacher, bow deeply, turn his back and recite in a loud singsong voice. All the boys studied aloud, so that a Chinese schoolroom of the old-fashioned sort was a very noisy place. If Yat-sen did not recite well, or if he was mischievous, the teacher reached out his ruler and slapped him on the palms of his hands.

How tired the boys were before the end of the long day! Yat-sen was especially restless. His whole body was full of energy and he longed to be outdoors, flying his kite or playing games. He had a rebellious heart, and it grew more rebellious because there was no escape from school. He learned easily to read and to write, his memory grew strong and he never forgot what he learned. But all the time inside his skull that roving mind of his was dreaming of getting away from the schoolroom, even from the village, and roaming the world.

It was easy for Yat-sen to make such dreams. Many of the villagers went away to America. In his own home were his two aunts, widows of his two uncles, his father's brothers, who had gone away to America to dig gold. News had come to the village in 1848 that gold had been discovered in California, and white men, who did not like the hard work of digging in the mines, wanted the Chinese men to come and do the digging for them. The white men promised high wages, and steamship companies sent white men to the Sun village to tell the wonders of California, to show maps and promise steamer tickets. Father Sun's two young brothers were among those who went early, leaving their wives behind them. The family waited and waited, but the men never came home again, and long afterwards the waiting wives heard that one husband had died at sea and the other in a California gold field.

By 1851, fifteen years before Yat-sen was even

born, there were twenty-five thousand Chinese working in California, not only in mining but at all sorts of labor, and they were good workers. When Yat-sen was still small, his older brother Ah-mei decided to leave home, too, and go to Hawaii where he heard business was good. So at home with Yat-sen was only his younger sister, who could not be much company to him because she was having her feet bound and could not run about. Yat-sen said, years later, that when he remembered his boyhood at home he seemed to hear always the sound of his sister crying because her feet hurt her so much. Perhaps even then he wished that girls need not suffer this pain, and perhaps he made up his mind to change this, too, someday.

Certainly he was a courageous, brave, independent boy, and he kept on wishing that he could see the world instead of going to school, year after year, and then having to work hard on the farm to help his father. When he was ten years old, his brother Ah-mei came home for a visit, and made life harder by telling fine stories of how well he was getting on in Hawaii. By now he had some land of his own, and he was planning to buy a small store in a village. He brought back money and gifts, and the farmhouse began to look prosperous. He saw Yat-sen listening to everything, and he knew how the boy longed to wander.

"Let me take my little brother back with me," he said to their parents. "He can help me in the shop and on my own farm."

"No," Father Sun said. "This boy must go to school. He is clever, and we will give him a good education."

"He can go to school in Honolulu," Ah-mei said. "We have a fine school there called Iolani. A good bishop is in charge, and he takes care of the boys."

"No," Mother Sun said. "Yat-sen is too young to leave home."

He hid among the passengers crowded in the hold

The two brothers said no more then, but when Ah-mei was alone with him, Yat-sen said, "I will run away from home, Ah-mei."

Ah-mei said, "I will help you."

The two brothers then planned a scheme whereby Yat-sen would leave home secretly and stow away on some ship that was taking Chinese to Hawaii to work on the sugar plantations there.

So it happened. When Yat-sen was still only twelve years old, he left home and went to Hongkong, a port by the sea. There he found a ship ready to sail to Hawaii, and he hid himself among the passengers crowded in the hold. Nobody discovered him, or perhaps they thought he was just one of the children of a passenger. When Yat-sen reached Hawaii, his brother took care of him and soon put him into Iolani, or the Bishop's School, where all the teachers except one were English. There the Chinese boy had to learn to speak the new language.

Three years Yat-sen spent in the school, and at first he must have been happy there, for the records show no new rebellions or mischief for a while. He enjoyed his work, especially in science and music. He found that he had a pleasant singing voice, and he liked to sing in the choir. Then his rebellious heart began stirring in him again. Iolani was a Christian school, and all the pupils had to learn the principles of this religion. Since Christians had developed science, Yat-sen thought he would like to be a Christian, too, and so he went to his brother and told him.

"Ah-mei, I wish to be a Christian."

How angry Ah-mei was when he heard those words!

"How can you be a Christian?" he shouted. "It is a foreign religion, and it is not the religion of our ancestors. It is time for you to go home to our parents. It is time for you to be married and settle down. I am sorry I ever brought you here."

17

Yat-sen finished school with prizes and honors that same year, and then Ah-mei put him on a steamer and sent him home. He could not be responsible for a younger brother who was so rebellious as to want to be a Christian.

2

The Broken Gods

YAT-SEN AT NEARLY SIXTEEN WAS NOT AT ALL the same boy who had left the family farmhouse a few years before. He had learned American ways in Honolulu while he was studying English and science in the Bishop's School, and he saw the Hawaiians themselves giving up many of their old superstitions. When he came home and found his own family still believing in the gods in the temples, he grew very angry with them. The whole

19

village, he decided, was backward and ignorant of science, and he believed that the people's superstitious religion was what had made them so.

What a trouble he became to his family now! They were always fearful of what he would do and say, and they were constantly embarrassed by his refusal to take part in the family rites and customs. Worst of all, there was another boy in the village who was almost as bad, a boy named Liu Hao-tung. His father had been a businessman in Shanghai and there Hao-tung had gone to school and had learned to be a Christian. When he was sixteen his father died, and Hao-tung as the eldest son brought the body back to the ancestral graveyard in the village. Thus he met Yat-sen, who was anxious to find just such a friend. The two young men talked together, and together they decided to change the village.

Yat-sen told Hao-tung, "China must have a new government, a true Chinese government of good men who will care for our people and build schools and hospitals and railroads and make our old country strong again."

It was a wonderful dream for the two young friends, and they could not wait to make it come true. They decided to begin at once here in their own village where they saw ignorance and superstition a-plenty. Even their own families thought that sickness and trouble came from the gods in the temples, and they tried to please the gods by gifts and prayers.

One day Yat-sen could bear it no longer. It was a festival day, and the people were gathered in the temple with the priests. Suddenly he got up and began to talk.

"These gods are no gods!" he cried. "How can they protect our village when they cannot even protect themselves? Look!"

To the horror of the watching crowd, while Hao-tung stood by him, he broke off the fingers

To their horror he struck an image in the face

of one of the images and struck another in the face. Of course the lacquered clay figures could make no response, but the people were terrified. What would happen to them now? This bold and impious boy must be sent away. Father Sun hurried home, and he and Mother Sun decided that their rebellious younger son must leave home at once. He must go to school again and learn how to make his living away from the village. Thus it was that Yat-sen was sent to Hongkong, the British Crown colony, and Hao-tung went back to Shanghai.

In a few months good Father Sun died unexpectedly. There must have been whisperings in the village that this was the punishment upon the family for the rebel son. At any rate, Yat-sen who had come home for the funeral was still not welcome, and he went back to Hongkong again when the period of mourning was over. This time he went to Queens College and began to study hard. Though this was an English preparatory school, it was the rule that Chinese pupils must study Chinese, year by year, while they studied English. Yat-sen thus was trained in his own language, and it was a great benefit to him later.

That was a strange year for the eager high-spirited boy. His father's death had made him sad and perhaps more tender than he had been to his family. When his mother wrote him that the family had decided that he must be married soon, he said nothing. It was the custom for a young man to marry a young woman whom his family selected for him. So Yat-sen went home again, this time for his wedding, and allowed himself to be married to a girl he had never seen. After the wedding feast and the ceremonies, he went back to school. His wife lived with his mother in the family home and helped in the house and was a good and dutiful member of the Sun family.

His determination to live his own life grew strong. The best way to show his independence, Yat-sen thought, was to become a baptized Christian. An American missionary named Charles Hager became his friend, and was much help to the lonely young man as he decided upon this step. Yat-sen took his new religion with great earnestness and immediately began to persuade his Chinese schoolmates to be Christians, too. This was, he told them, the quickest way to show their determination to break with old-fashioned ways.

The news reached Ah-mei, who was paying for Yat-sen's schooling, and how angry that elder brother became! "Unless you give up this foreign religion," he wrote, "I shall send no more money home for you."

Now a real quarrel began between the two brothers. Yat-sen would not give up his religion, and Ah-mei could do nothing with him. In the China of those days the elder brother had authority over the family after the father died, and so Ah-mei had the right to demand obedience. But Yat-sen steadily refused. Ah-mei took him out of school and brought him to Honolulu, pretending that Yat-sen's name had to be signed for the sale of some property that belonged to them both. After Yat-sen had signed the papers, Ah-mei was still angry. He would not help his younger brother unless he gave up his new religion, and this

Yat-sen would not do. Now he was stranded in the foreign city, and he would not have known how to live except that Chinese Christians there took pity on him and collected enough money to send him back to China.

All during this experience, Yat-sen was trying to decide how he could best help his country. How could he persuade his fellow citizens to rise up and demand a government of their own and make a better life for themselves? He thought perhaps he ought to become a preacher and go about the countryside telling people of his new religion, for Christianity always made people want to be free. When he returned to Hongkong, however, there was no school of theology to teach him how to be a preacher. So he decided to be a doctor. As a good doctor, he could help many people.

His American friend, Charles Hager, gave him a letter to a famous American missionary doctor, Dr. John Kerr, saying that Yat-sen was an unusual

The three young men often talked in secret

young man and deserved help. Dr. Kerr took Yat-sen into his great hospital in Canton and there he stayed for a year, studying and working his way by jobs in the hospital. Now he was really independent, and to add to his joy his old friend, Liu Hao-tung, came to the hospital, too, to study medicine. The two friends shared a room and soon they had a third friend, Cheng Shih-liang. This young man was from Shanghai also, and he was filled with bitterness because his father had died from the effects of a lawsuit in which an unjust magistrate had decided against him. Shih-liang was angry at the corruption of government officials, and the three young men often talked in secret of what they would do to help their country, so weakened by the selfish rulers.

"We are actually in danger," Hao-tung exclaimed. "Any foreign power can attack us as the French did, and we could not resist."

It was true. China had no defense forces. And it

was true that France had attacked China in order to seize Tongking, the link between Indo-China, which she already possessed, and the rich province of Yunnan, which she longed to occupy as a place for trade. The Chinese soldiers had resisted bravely, but they could do nothing when the French warships stormed up the coast even as far as the city of Foochow in the coastal province of Fukien. It was not only the loss of Chinese territory that made the young rebels so bitter. Yat-sen was sure that while the Chinese soldiers were trying to fight for their country, the Manchu government in Peking was making a disgraceful peace.

"But where can we begin?" he exclaimed to his two friends.

Shih-liang had the answer. "In the old secret societies," he said. And then he told Yat-sen that there had been among the Chinese for many years old anti-Manchu secret societies, whose members were men determind to get back their own country. He himself, Shih-liang said, belonged to one of these societies, called "The Triad."

The three friends did not stay together very long. Yat-sen wanted to begin at once to help his countrymen. His brother was willing to be friendly again now that Yat-sen had decided not to be a preacher of the Christian religion, and he sent money to enable him to enter the new medical school at a great English hospital newly opened in Hongkong. There Yat-sen went, glad to be in the free air of that city under British rule. Now he worked hard at his education while he dreamed of the future. In five years he graduated with high honors. As usual, he made a faithful friend during these years, an Englishman, one of the founders of the hospital, whose name was Dr. James Cantlie, afterwards Sir James Cantlie. That name he was never to forget, for to Dr. Cantlie he was to owe his life in the years to come.

3

The Revolutionist

"YOU ARE A BORN SURGEON," DR. CANTLIE SAID TO Sun Yat-sen after graduation. "You must go on with surgery."

"If I do," Yat-sen replied, "will you help me when I need you?"

"I will," Dr. Cantlie replied.

With that promise, Yat-sen went to the Portuguese colonial city of Macao, the nearest large city to his own village. Here he took over an entire building from an old-fashioned Chinese hospital and set up his own surgery. It was now 1892 and he was twenty-five years old. His first child was already born, a boy, known afterwards as Sun Fo.

Sun Yat-sen was the first surgeon in the city, and he had many patients. But people still distrusted foreign medical methods, and when he operated he had to allow the friends and the families of the patient to watch every move. When he felt an operation was too dangerous for him to undertake alone, he sent for Dr. Cantlie, and this famous old surgeon always came to help.

"Why did I go to Macao to help this man?" Dr. Cantlie said later. "For the same reason that others have fought and died for Sun Yat-sen—because I loved and respected him."

The hospital in Macao did not continue long, however, for Yat-sen found he must have a Portuguese certificate, and at twenty-six he did not wish to return to school again to get it. He decided that he would go to North China and try to find a place in a new hospital in Tientsin opened by the famous old Chinese Viceroy, Li Hung-chang.

The Viceroy had just returned in great magnificence from a trip around the world and now wanted to help his country to have modern institutions like the ones he had seen in other countries. Yat-sen had heard much about the Viceroy, and he dreamed of being taken into his employ and sharing in the plans for modernization. He prepared a memorial paper wherein he set forth his own ideas and plans for China. He hoped to be able to give it to Li Hung-chang in person. Alas, many young men were trying to get to the great man, and no one knew a humble Sun Yat-sen! He was given neither an interview nor a job, and he had to put his paper back in his pocket. His friend Hao-tung had come with him, sharing his hopes and dreams. It was all the harder to know they had failed because they heard of another young man whom

Li Hung-chang was encouraging and developing, Yuan Shih-kai, a big handsome fellow whose chief interest was in creating a modern army.

Nevertheless, it was good for Yat-sen to have put down on paper what he believed his country needed. He urged the development of China's natural resources in men, in agriculture, in mines and in trade. He wanted free public education and especially trade schools where boys might be taught about machinery and farming and building railroads and opening mines. Agriculture must be developed first, he said, so that the people could have more food. This program Sun Yat-sen never changed.

Still, there was nothing for him to do now but go back again to his profession. Yet somehow his heart was no longer in his work. To be a doctor was a slow way to help his country, too slow, trying to heal one sick person after another. He wanted to work quickly and fundamentally. The way to do this, he decided, was to reach the young and the strong and waken them to the dangers in which their weak country stood. Sooner or later, he was sure, China would be attacked by a stronger nation, for weakness invited attack.

He was right. In 1894 Japan attacked China in full force. Japan had modern weapons and China did not. The end was inevitable. Japan would win

In 1894 Japan attacked China in full force

and the war would be short. Yet a losing war, Yat-sen reasoned, might be his opportunity. His people might be angry enough, humiliated enough, frightened enough, to rise up and demand a change in government. Then would be his chance. He could lead the revolution into constructive and wise ways, and help to establish a true republican government, something like the American form of government. But this would cost money and he had none.

On a hot August day not long after the war began, Yat-sen made his final decision. He closed his hospital forever and gave himself wholly to the life he had planned for so long. He decided, first of all, to go to Honolulu and talk with the Chinese businessmen there and persuade them to give him money for the cause. And he took his paper out of his desk, that paper which he had not been able to give to Li Hung-chang. He sent it to a progressive newspaper in Shanghai for publication. There educated men would read it and learn to know his name and his ideas.

In Honolulu again, Yat-sen talked privately with the Chinese businessmen. He told them that their country was in grave danger.

"Selfishness was never more selfish," he declared passionately. "The whole nation is confused. Nobody understands! There is nobody to save the situation. How then is calamity to be averted? If we do not make the effort to hold our own, if we do not rouse ourselves in time, our thousands of years of fame and culture, our many years of traditions and morals, will be destroyed and utterly ruined. Who must be responsible in this situation? Who else but good and responsible men who know what the situation is?"

Sun Yat-sen was a born orator. His straight, slender figure, his thin square face, his burning and fearless eyes, impressed all who saw him, and when he spoke his deep and ardent voice was irresistible.

But most convincing of all was his honesty. Integrity shone from his every look, and it was clear to all that here was an unselfish man, devoted to the freedom of his country and the benefit of his people.

One after another of the Chinese in Honolulu came forward to help him. In that same year he established his first patriotic society, the Hsing Chung Huei, or Prosper China Society. He was its first initiate. He placed his hand on an open Bible and swore allegiance to the aims and principles of the society, and then he signed the register. A small number of men, all young, joined with him and bound themselves to work for a new China, a nation modern and strong enough to stand against any enemy. Branches of the society were to be established anywhere in the world where there were as many as fifteen persons who wished to join. The head office was to be in China. Money, of course, was the first need, and each member was asked to give ten dollars, with the hope that it might be only a loan and might one day be returned with interest by a strong new government.

Among those who listened in Honolulu was Ah-mei. He was frightened by Japan's attack on China, by the obvious helplessness of the people and by the treachery of the government. He was a prosperous man now, and he did not want to see his country lost. He put his hand deep into his pocket and pulled out a generous sum. At last he believed that his brother was right.

Sun Yat-sen now began the life of an active revolutionist.

"Revolutions are not made in the interests of individuals," he wrote. "They are the result of the revolutionary action of the masses. Washington and Napoleon were by no means the chief factors in the American and French Revolutions. When the Americans found the English yoke unbearable, they invited Washington to be their leader and rose in revolt. In France it was already after the Revolution that Bonaparte emerged to take power into his own hands. Both these men were raised up by the wave of revolution."

Sun Yat-sen believed that he, too, was a man thrown up by the wave of revolution. What is revolution, he asked, but the determination of a people, long oppressed by poverty and discontent and despair, to change their state? What they want in its place is not always clear, but one thing they know, that what they have is intolerable. It was inevitable, Sun Yat-sen believed, that when people reach this point they choose the man to lead them in the struggle. He believed himself to be this man in China, and with a solemn sense of duty and with single-hearted devotion he prepared himself for leadership.

Yet he was not the first man to declare that China must change if she was to survive in the modern world. For centuries certain brave and learned men had been critics of corrupt and ignorant rulers. Confucius himself had taught that a ruler should be concerned for his people as a father is concerned for his children. Yet, as always, brave and learned men were few. Most of the classical scholars were dependent upon the government for position and livelihood, for those who passed high in the imperial examinations were almost always chosen as officials. While they knew the principles of good government, they did not dare to insist upon their practice, and they were fond of quoting an old proverb which said, "To know is easy but to do is hard." This they made their excuse for inaction, and against the excuse the few brave and learned had declared themselves long before Sun Yat-sen was born. Yen Yuan, for example, had early said, "What I want is motion, activity, reality!" and Li Kung, decades later, pressed for knowledge based on experience and research in every field of knowledge. Hsu Shih-chang in his great work, *The Lives and Work of the Ching Scholars*, pointed out that the chief concern of the best of these scholars, though only the best, was to persuade rulers to put into practice whole-hearted reforms in the government and for the people.

Such scholars began to read Western books and to learn of Western achievements. They were interested in the whole world as well as in their own country. By their writing and talking they did indeed spread discontent among the people, and this discontent did indeed build up into that wave of revolution of which Sun Yat-sen felt himself to be the crest.

There were two schools of thought, however, among the revolutionists. One believed that the monarchy must be preserved, and reforms brought about through its power. This group was led by Yuan Shih-kai, that same young man so favored by the Viceroy Li Kung-chang. The other group, led by Sun Yat-sen, believed that emperors never reform themselves and must be overthrown and a new government representing the people be set up. These two men, Yuan Shih-kai and Sun Yat-sen, were to oppose each other to the bitter end of their separate lives.

The division went straight up to the highest places. Yuan Shih-kai rose to great influence at the Manchu court as Premier. He knew about his opponent, Sun Yat-sen, and kept watch on all his movements.

Before Sun could be entirely free to pursue his dangerous and solitary path, he had to endure the pain of seeing his decision bring trouble to his family. From Honolulu he had planned to go straight to the United States, there to continue his organization of Chinese patriots among the overseas Chinese. Before he could do so, he had a letter from a friend in Shanghai, whose surname was Soong and whose name was Charles Jones. This name, Charles, strange for a Chinese, Soong had taken for himself many years before, when he was a cabin boy on an American ship. The Captain, Charles Jones, was attracted to the cheerful and lively young Chinese who served him. Knowing him to have unusual intelligence, he decided to help him to find American friends who would give him an education. This he did, and years later Charles Soong returned to his own country and became a successful and wealthy businessman in Shanghai. He was friendly to the revolutionary movement and especially to Sun Yat-sen. Now, because the Japanese were very dangerously near to victory in the war with China, he urged Sun Yat-sen to come home and start the revolution at once, lest China be defeated.

Instead then of going westward, Sun Yat-sen gathered some of his group together and went to Hongkong. There he set up a shop which was really an office. From this place they could plot to buy ammunition, dynamite and weapons as well as recruit men. But the war with Japan ended abruptly. China was defeated and forced to cede the rich and beautiful island of Formosa to Japan and to acknowledge the independence of Korea, which up to this time had been a dependency of China. This meant that Japan planned to annex Korea, and she proceeded to do so.

The defeat brought no peace or comfort to China. Soldiers, dismissed from the army, wandered lost over the countryside, robbing and despoiling. The government did nothing to help them or the people. Now more than ever, Sun Yat-sen felt, the revolution must be organized. He worked harder and recruited more and more men.

Suddenly, in September 1895, the plot was discovered. A consignment of six hundred pistols in barrels labeled "cement" was discovered by the British Maritime Customs. Sun's headquarters were immediately raided. Five of his men were caught and killed, and seventy more were arrested. The first man to die was Sun Yat-sen's old friend, Liu Hao-tung, who had been with him from the first and had worked so faithfully with him. It was the beginning of the grim sacrifices that the revolution demanded, and it was one that weighed hard on Sun Yat-sen's heart and was never to be forgotten.

He himself escaped and was hidden by friends in Canton. Then escaping again, he went wandering on foot through the labyrinth of canals and inlets of the Pearl River Delta, that historic home of pirate bands. No one recognized the disheveled, poorly dressed man. He headed for Macao by boat and on foot, only to see on the city gate as he entered it a poster offering a huge reward for his capture. He decided to leave Macao and go to Hongkong. There he sought out his old friend, Dr. Cantlie, who advised him to go to a lawyer, and see what claims he could make for protection by the British. No claims could be made, the lawyer declared, and the best thing to do was to take in-

Sun Yat-sen's headquarters were immediately raided

stant flight and go as far as he could. "Although,"
the lawyer said, "Peking's arm is still a long one,
and in whatever part of the world you go you must
expect to hear of the Manchu government."

Now Sun Yat-sen knew that until he was successful in his purpose and a new government set up
in his country, he must live as a fugitive, doing his
work in secret. He left Hongkong and went to
Japan. This called for disguise. He cut off the long
queue, which every Chinese man wore then. This
was a revolutionary step in itself, since the queue
was the sign of subjection to the Manchus. He
grew a moustache and bought a suit of modern Japanese garments. Then he looked in the mirror and
was astonished to see himself. He was darker in
coloring than most Chinese and really looked now
like a Japanese. As a Japanese he was safe, for they
were the conquerors and were not to be molested.

When he left Japan and went once more to
Hawaii, Yat-sen found his brother in deep distress.

After the plot had been discovered, the family in the ancestral home in the village near Canton was immediately in danger. It was an old Chinese and Manchu custom to punish the family of a revolutionist, especially if he himself could not be found. Swift flight for the family was the only safety. The anxious and good-hearted Ah-mei immediately sent money for them to come at once to Hawaii. There Sun Yat-sen found them all, including his wife and children. His old mother reproached him sadly for the uprooting. "Oh, why," she moaned, "did you bring all this trouble on your family?"

Sun Yat-sen could never make her understand the dedication of a man to the cause of his country, but this, too, he must bear. The danger for the family was very real. This was proved when a kindly villager, who helped the family to get away, was thrown into prison. His son, also a rich businessman in Hawaii, could not get him released, even for vast sums of money. Only after six years had passed did the Chinese Minister in Washington finally get the old man free again.

A revolutionist sacrifices not only himself but his family and his friends, but by now Sun Yat-sen knew the cost and accepted it. From now on he was seldom with his wife and his children, and Ah-mei took care of them as best he could. Sun Yat-sen was lonely and free.

4

A Hunted Man

HE DECIDED NEXT TO CARRY OUT HIS EARLIER plans to go to the United States, England and Europe in order to meet with Chinese in all countries and to gather money and men and begin the revolution again.

One day in 1896, just before he left, he saw upon a street in Honolulu, his old friends, Dr. and Mrs. Cantlie, with their children and a Japanese nurse. He spoke to them, but they did not recognize him. The nurse actually spoke to him in Japanese, so complete was his disguise. Sun Yat-sen smiled and introduced himself, but he did not stay long to talk. When Dr. Cantlie told him they were on their way to London, Sun Yat-sen said, "Ah, I shall meet you there!" and went his way. It was a casual meeting but an important one, a lucky coincidence such as often occurred in Sun Yat-sen's life.

He left soon after this for San Francisco and entered without difficulty because he looked so Japanese. For three months he traveled everywhere in America, gathering Chinese together secretly and telling them of the desperate plight of their country. He urged them to organize and give money and men to overthrow the despotic and selfish Manchu government and set up a republic like the Republic of the United States. It was hard work, and he was often discouraged.

"Though I worked very hard," he said, "there were very few who paid any attention to me. There were only a few individuals, at most a dozen or two in each city, who were favorable to my ideas of revolution."

He felt safe, traveling about in what seemed to be complete secrecy and obscurity. What he did not know was that the Chinese Minister in Washington knew of his entry at San Francisco. The Minister had hired detectives to follow him everywhere, report his movements, and send descriptions of him and even to find a photograph which Sun Yat-sen unwisely had taken of himself for friends in San Francisco. When Sun Yat-sen later sailed for London, the Chinese Minister in Washington wrote to the Chinese Minister in London, giving orders that Sun Yat-sen was to be followed by detectives. The British government must be asked to give him up on the grounds that he was a political criminal, and he must be returned to China to be beheaded for trying to overthrow the government in Peking.

The Chinese Minister in London obeyed as best he could. He had Sun Yat-sen followed, but the British government refused to give him up, saying that they had no treaty with China requiring this. Meanwhile for ten pleasant days Sun Yat-sen went freely about the great interesting city of London. He called often upon his friends Dr. and Mrs. Cant-lie, whose home was in Portland Place, not far from the Chinese Legation.

One Sunday morning when he was on his way to Dr. Cantlie's home to go to church with the family, a Chinese spoke to him on the street. After a few minutes of friendly talk he led Sun toward the Legation building and invited him to come in and look around. Everyone was cordial, and he was shown the entire building, even up to the third floor. There as he entered a room, the door closed

When the lock turned, he knew he was a prisoner

suddenly behind him. At this instant he realized
that he had been too innocent, for he saw facing
him a tall Englishman, whose face was cold. It was
Sir Halliday Macartney, British adviser to the Chinese Legation.

"We have heard of you," Sir Halliday said
sternly. "Word has been sent to us from America
that a political prisoner, named Sun, left there for

England. You are certainly that man. It is necessary for us to detain you here until we can communicate with Peking and receive instructions concerning you."

No use, Sun Yat-sen saw, in trying to move that cold-hearted man!

"How long will this be?" he asked.

"Until the expense of a ship chartered to take you back can be authorized," the Englishman replied.

He opened the door and went out. In that brief instant Sun Yat-sen saw armed guards stationed outside. Then the door was closed, and he heard the lock turned.

He was a prisoner!

What hope was there now? He was a prisoner and alone. No one even knew he was in London except Dr. Cantlie, and there was no way of reaching that one friend he had. The door did not open except to admit an English servant, bringing food three times a day and coal for the meager fire. Alone Sun pondered upon his probable fate. If the Legation officials succeeded in sending him back to China, he would be tortured and then executed in the old traditional way of punishing traitors. Yet he was a patriot and not a traitor.

He could not eat or sleep. The days dragged by and the time drew near when inevitably the cable must come from the Imperial government in Peking authorizing the money needed for chartering a ship to take him home. What could he do? He prayed desperately to God. He wrote letters on any bit of paper he could find and dropped them out of the window, weighted with the coins he had in his pockets when he was arrested. Through a Cantonese interpreter who came in occasionally to translate for him to the servants or to the Legation officials, he tried to reach Dr. Cantlie, but the interpreter was too frightened to help him.

At last Sun Yat-sen decided to appeal to the manservant. The man was, he said, a Christian, and in the name of his religion Sun Yat-sen persuaded him. Just as the Sultan of Turkey wished to kill all the Christians, he told the man, so the Emperor of China wished to kill him because he was a Christian. "My life is in your hands," he told the simple frightened fellow. "If you let the matter be known outside, I shall be saved; if not, I shall certainly be executed."

Sun Yat-sen spoke with terrible earnestness, yet with deep calm. He had prayed for many days, and on the morning of the day before, Friday, October the eighteenth, it had seemed to him that his prayer was to be answered. He rose from his knees with a new conviction. Somehow, this time he was successful where before he had not prevailed. When Sun spoke as a Christian, the man dared not refuse. He promised to think it over which he did to the extent of going home and telling his wife.

The result was that near midnight the next day, Saturday, October 19, 1896, the doorbell rang at the Cantlie home. When Dr. Cantlie opened the door himself, no one was there, but a note lay on the step.

The servant's wife, being less fearful and perhaps a warmer Christian, had decided that if her husband dared not warn Dr. Cantlie, she would do so.

Dr. Cantlie picked up the note and read it. "There is a friend of yours imprisoned in the Chinese Legation. They intend sending him to China, where it is certain they will hang him. It is very sad for the poor man and unless something is done at once, he will be taken away and no one will know it. I dare not sign my name, but this is the truth, so believe what I say. Whatever you do must be done at once or it will be too late. His name is, I believe, Sin Yin Sen."

Now Dr. Cantlie knew where his young Chinese friend had gone! For days the Cantlies had wondered why Sun had so suddenly disappeared. Knowing in what danger he lived, they had not tried to find him.

"Had that humble woman failed in her purpose," Dr. Cantlie said afterwards, "the regeneration of China would have been thrown back indefinitely, for the reformer would have lost his life and the Manchus would still be in power."

As it was, Dr. Cantlie wasted not a moment. He went at once to Scotland Yard, although now it was half-past one in the early morning, and reported Sun Yat-sen's case. He found the inspector in charge indifferent.

"Go home and keep quiet," the man said. "It is none of your business or ours."

Dr. Cantlie could only go home and wait for dawn. Early again he went to Scotland Yard, accompanied this time by an English friend, Sir Patrick Manson, and reported to another inspector.

The inspector said there had already been a report made in the night by a "drunk, excited sort of fellow," and that nothing could be done. The fellow was, of course, Dr. Cantlie himself who might have been expected to be excited but certainly was not drunk.

Scotland Yard would do nothing, and now Dr. Cantlie wrote to the newspapers, hoping that publicity would help Sun Yat-sen. *The Times*, however, refused to publish this report when he appeared with it that Sunday night. On Monday morning Dr. Cantlie went to the British Foreign Office. There red tape began to unwind. An attempt to get an order to free Sun Yat-sen was thrown out by a judge at the Old Bailey Court. Dr. Cantlie by this time was really desperate. He hired a detective to sit in a cab and watch the door of the Chinese Legation, so that he would know if Sun Yat-sen were spirited away. Then a correspondent for another newspaper, *The Globe*, heard

Newsmen crowded into the Legation to get the story

rumors of what was going on and Dr. Cantlie gave him an interview. The story was published Thursday evening, and soon afterwards newspapermen crowded into the Chinese Legation, demanding the full story. Public criticism was aroused, and Sir Halliday Macartney knew that the plot could not be carried out.

By this time the Prime Minister himself, Lord Salisbury, was ready to intervene. He sent a courteous note to the Chinese Minister, saying that Sun's detention was contrary to British law, and advising him to release the prisoner.

On the next day, the British Foreign Office sent messengers to the Chinese Legation and Sun Yat-sen was handed over to them, a free man again. Dr. Cantlie took him home to rest and recuperate. The next day, only a few hours too late, the Chinese Legation received a cable from Peking telling them to spend the money to ship Sun Yat-sen back to China for punishment as a traitor.

5

A Troubled People

A FREE MAN? SUN YAT-SEN KNEW HE WOULD never be free again unless he was victorious. Wherever he went, in whatever house he stayed, asleep or awake, among friends or enemies, he was a marked man with a price upon his head. Often he had to travel in disguise as a peddler or a laborer. For seventeen years he was to face constant danger to his life. Once in Nanking when he was hiding on a junk, a man came into his cabin and said that he had been offered five thousand dollars to take him captive. Sun Yat-sen reasoned with him quietly and explained to him that his whole purpose was to save their country and make it a better place for the people. The man listened and fell to his knees and begged his forgiveness. Then he went out and hanged himself for even thinking of betraying such a man as Sun Yat-sen.

Once when Sun was hiding in a cabin outside the city of Canton, soldiers were sent to shoot him, but fishermen protected him until the soldiers themselves were shot.

Once on the island of Hainan he was compelled to live for six months in a small house, never going outside, until friends and neighbors helped him to escape.

Once in Canton two young government officials with a band of soldiers entered a house where he was hidden. They were determined to seize him, for his capture or his death would bring them great

The man fell to his knees and begged forgiveness

rewards. Sun met them calmly and took up one of the sacred books from his table and began to read aloud. His would-be captors asked him questions, and in the end, afraid of his goodness, they went away and left him.

Many times was he to save his own life in the years to come, not by fighting for himself, not by deserting his cause, but by the sheer power of his high integrity, which men could not doubt, and by the indomitable force of his personality.

For the Chinese people life was steadily growing worse. After the weakening war with Japan, four other powers took advantage of China's defeat to gain benefits for themselves. Germany took the port of Tsingtao in North China. Russia took Port Arthur in Manchuria; England took Weihaiwei in North China; and France took Kwangchow-wan. These and other European powers began to discuss dividing the whole of China into spheres of influence, where they would have special privileges in trade and power. This of course would mean final possession of China. In like fashion a century before, India had become a colonial possession of England.

The government in Peking was too weak to prevent the encroachment. The old Emperor was dead, the young Emperor was only twenty-seven years old. The Empress Dowager, the real ruler, was an ignorant and selfish woman who had spent the money the people had collected for a modern navy. With this money she had built a vast marble pleasure boat in the lake near the Summer Palace.

All thinking Chinese grew frightened of what might now happen to the country. Chang Chih-tung, the Viceroy of two of China's largest provinces, Hunan and Hupeh, wrote a book entitled *A Charge to Learn*. In it he said, "What will become of us? If we do not change soon, we shall become the slaves of the Westerners."

The young Emperor, influenced by good and intelligent men who were his teachers, gave his open approval to the book, and he sent out edicts advocating wide reforms. Schools of Western learning must be set up, he said, railroads must be built, the government itself must be reformed. Alas for this young and idealistic man!

Yuan Shih-kai, the Premier, did not want to lose

his place as he must if the government were overthrown. So he told the Empress Dowager secretly of the Emperor's plans. The Empress acted quickly and strongly. The Emperor's teachers were beheaded, except for two who escaped, Kang Yu-wei and Liang Chi-chao, and the Emperor was made a prisoner in his own luxurious palace. Life went on as it had before.

And where was Sun Yat-sen in these times? He was preparing quietly for the future, strengthening his mind and body for the leadership which he was to undertake in earnest. He was still in London, spending hours in the British Museum, reading and studying history and economics, government, agriculture and land reform, railroads and industry—everything which would be useful later for his own people. He wanted everything at once for his people.

In England and in the countries of Europe the struggles for a democratic government and better social conditions were separate efforts. They had taken hundreds of years and were still far from finished. But to Sun Yat-sen nothing was impossible. He wanted a democratic government and improved social conditions in China all at the same time. Two years he spent in study in England and in travel to Europe, to see for himself what the Western countries had done. Then, ready to work, he went back to his own part of the world, stopping only a little while in Honolulu to see his family on the way.

Japan was to be his base. Tens of thousands of young Chinese were there studying and working, for now Japan had become a place for hope, in spite of victory in the war and perhaps even because of it. Japan, a country of Asia, had in a short while become a modern power. She was building modern schools, hospitals, railroads, an army and a navy. In the government liberals had the power. Two great liberal leaders, Inukai and Okuma, were ready to be Sun's friends. They invited him to Tokyo, where he talked with them for many hours, "as if," he said, "we were old and intimate friends."

From Japan Sun returned, heavily disguised as he always was now, to a divided China and a troubled people. Outwardly everything went on as usual. Farmers planted their crops and harvested them. The cities were busy with small business and big shops. Young people grew up in their old-fashioned families, were married, had children and took their place in society. In Peking the Empress Dowager still ruled as a despot, determined to keep China what it had been for the last two hundred years. She was a proud and able woman but she was ignorant and opinionated, unable to believe what she did not want to believe. And she did not want to believe that the whole world was changing, that the modern West could no longer be held off, and that China must change, too, if it was to remain a sovereign nation.

Where could Sun Yat-sen look for help? Most of the old scholars, who were called the *literati*, were still supporters of the Empire. They had been well treated, and according to ancient custom they were given posts in government when they passed the Imperial examinations. Many of them had never been abroad or seen Western countries. It was hard for them to believe that China could not go on in the comfortable old ways. Yet there were a few among them who were now fearful. These were the brave men of integrity, and especially those who had been abroad. The government was not checking the greed of foreign nations and, to avoid trouble, much of China's national treasure and resources were being yielded too easily to their demands. Russia in 1896 was given land in Manchuria and the right to build a railway to Siberia. Germans had the rights to build railroads in the great northern province of Shantung. French and

Belgians had the rights to a vast trunk line railroad which stretched across the whole country from Hankow to Peking.

Many Chinese, especially the educated ones, were much disturbed by all this. Foreigners, they said, should not own the nation's railroads; for this meant that foreigners had control of shipping and travel, and trade would be in their hands. Yet most scholars and intellectuals did not know what to do. They could not change the mind of the Empress Dowager, and they, too, did not want to foster a revolution which might destroy a regime favorable to them.

Sun Yat-sen came fresh from Japan with his mind full of ideas and the inspiration of knowing what that vigorous country had done. Soon he saw that his help could not come from the entrenched scholars of his own country. He must look elsewhere for men and money. Now he remembered the advice of Chen Shih-liang, his friend of their student days in Canton. And he turned to the secret societies.

To understand China one must understand the place of the secret societies through the past centuries. China was more than once conquered by a foreign people. When this happened the Chinese people, having no army or navy, seemed always to yield. They never did yield actually. The seeds of their revolt were always hidden in the secret societies. The members of these societies were patriotic men who bided their time, but kept alive among themselves the old Chinese ways and philosophies.

While the foreign conquerors were strong, the secret societies went underground. They waited for time to pass, for the conquerors to grow weak, as surely they always did, waited until the chance came to take China back again for the Chinese. They had taken China back after the Mongols had held her for centuries. During the Chinese dynasty of the Mings, they had been inactive, but they had never dissolved. The Ming emperors, grown weak with power and success in their time, were overthrown again by a foreign aggressor, the Manchus from the north. Immediately the secret societies strengthened themselves. The day would come, they knew from centuries of history, when they would be needed once more to free their country.

Who were these men of the patriotic secret societies? They were now plain men, not scholars, not even learned. The scholars had withdrawn from the societies, unwilling to risk the loss of the benefits they were receiving from the Manchu invaders. But the poor and ignorant were receiving no benefits. As times grew worse, such men flocked to the societies, hoping for a chance to overthrow the dynasty and start a new and better one of their own. This was the pattern of ancient Chinese society, and it had persisted for thousands of years. It was a sort of rough practical democracy. To these men Sun Yat-sen now turned for help.

There was another small but very devoted group among the revolutionaries. Chinese scholars, the men of literature and art, scorned the young graduates of the Christian missionary schools. These young people, they said, had no real education or culture. They did not understand the classic Chinese books, nor could they recite the ancient poetry. They knew only the crude rudiments of Western science and languages. What these dignified gentlemen did not understand was that in Christian missionary schools young men and women had studied Western history and had learned of the bitter struggle for freedom which had gone on in most Western countries. They read of the War for Independence in America, they followed the long path of the people's struggle for freedom in Britain. Magna Carta meant something to these young Chinese, and the cry of Liberty, Equality and Fraternity in the French Revolution shook their own hearts. Above all, in the Christian religion they learned of the value of the individual, and the right of every human being to be free and equal to every other in God's sight. Christianity itself was and is the world's most tremendous revolutionary force.

When these young men and women graduated from the mission schools, they found there was no real place for them in the nation's life. The government did not trust them, the people did not like them. Yet they were a young, patriotic, zealous group, trained to work for their people. Missionaries had taught them that they must be willing to sacrifice themselves for others, but they did not know how or where to begin. It was natural and inevitable that they found their leader in Sun Yat-sen, himself a Christian and the graduate of a missionary school.

Before Sun Yat-sen could organize his forces, however, there was a violent outbreak in China against the Western peoples. The encroachments of one country after another had inflamed the people and had incensed the aging Empress. She did not know where to turn. China had no modern army or navy, and for this she was now to blame. She had squandered the nation's money, and she feared the angry people would overthrow her government. In her desperation she turned to a group of fanatical and ignorant men, who called themselves the Boxers. They claimed to be superhuman, and they told her that they would kill all the foreigners in the country if she would give them permission. They said they had magic powers, and foreign bullets could not penetrate their flesh. They even gave a demonstration before the old Empress, using trickery to protect their bodies from bullets.

It was just the easy sort of way that she sought. She sent out an edict against the foreigners of all

The Boxers led a nationwide massacre of white people

nations, commanding that on a certain date the nation-wide massacre of white people must begin. With them, she commanded, the Chinese Christians also must be put to death.

In that summer of 1900 more than two hundred Americans and Europeans—men, women and little children—were killed and with them many hundreds of Chinese Christians. In Peking the foreign legations were besieged, and the allied troops of eight Western nations were sent swiftly to save them. When the Empress Dowager heard that foreign armies were marching on the capital she fled with her court across the mountains to the distant city of Si-an, complaining that she had to leave so quickly that she had no time to comb her hair or eat an egg.

Peking fell easily to the foreign armies, and the Chinese suffered terrible defeat. The soldiers looted the houses and palaces of the capital. The Western governments demanded such heavy payments in cash that it seemed unlikely China could ever finish paying. Never had China fallen so low. The people were stunned at the failure of the Boxers and the flight of the Imperial Court.

Now, Sun Yat-sen felt, was the time for him to come forward. He tried to land at Hongkong, but the British would not allow it. So he went instead to the island of Formosa, which was then under Japanese rule. He counted strongly on help from Japan, remembering how friendly the liberal government there had been to him. Meanwhile his old friend, Chen Shih-liang, had organized the secret societies. He said he had ten thousand men waiting to rise together against the government. In Formosa the Japanese Governor promised to help. Guns and ammunition were ordered from Japan. A revolt was organized even in the Viceroy's palace in Canton. The attack was to come from within and without at the same time.

Alas, during the very two weeks while the attack was being planned the Japanese government changed. A long struggle had been going on between the liberals and the conservatives in that country. When the reactionaries were swept into power in Japan, they sent orders immediately to the Governor of Formosa that no help was to be given to the revolutionist, Sun Yat-sen. Sun could only get the message to Chen Shih-liang, who quickly disbanded his forces and sent them underground again. The lonely revolt in the Viceroy's palace took place, since the men there did not know of the change of plan, and the leader was beheaded. It was Sun Yat-sen's second failure.

6

The Waiting Time

WHAT DID THE NEW FAILURE MEAN TO SUN YAT-sen? Simply that he must withdraw again and prepare more soundly. He went back to Japan and lived there secretly for more than three years. Sometimes he traveled to get men and money, but he spent most of the time alone studying and writing and organizing.

He made his headquarters in Yokohama, that busy modern seaport of Japan. He called himself

Mr. Nakagama, and he lived in a gloomy house in a dark back street of the Chinese quarter of the city. His room was plainly furnished with a few tables and chairs and many books. They were not books for amusement. They were books about history and political economy, about war and tactics and weapons, explosives and projectiles. He had maps, and he marked in red the places where his rebels had fought and where they had failed, only, he felt, because they had not got the ammunition he had been promised.

"We are not in the least depressed," he said. "In fact we are encouraged, for we see now how easily the Imperial troops can be defeated as soon as our men are properly armed and trained for the great effort."

It was impossible, he still believed, to carry out the needed reforms in China through the old government. "Anyone who knows the Chinese Court," he said, "and knows who surrounds the Emperor, knows that he is powerless."

Sun felt that his people were superior to the Japanese, more intelligent, more lively in mind, more strong in body and that China could do in fifteen years what Japan had taken thirty to do.

"It is a great ambition," he said, one day when he was talking to an American friend who had come to see him. He lit a cigar and puffed out great clouds of smoke as he walked about the room. Then he declared firmly, "It is worth giving one's life for."

Yet it is as important for a man to know when not to act as it is to know when to act. Sun Yat-sen felt that now was a time to wait. There was great ferment in China. After the terrible failure of the Boxers, all the people were beginning to feel that some sort of change must take place in government and life.

The Empress Dowager herself did not dare to bring her court back to Peking until she had shown that she too felt there must be a change. She put

"It is worth giving one's life for," he declared

out three edicts proclaiming that reforms were
necessary and that first of all there must be reform
in education. The old-fashioned eight-part essay
based upon the classics was no longer to be re-
quired. Instead, modern schools must be established, and so that there might be teachers enough,
students were to be sent abroad to study Western
methods. The trickle of students going abroad

increased after this to a great stream, sometimes hundreds a month. Japan received the first great overflow, for Japan was still the example for China —an Asian nation that had modernized herself in a generation. But students also began to go to America and England and France and Russia.

Sun Yat-sen waited. The reformers were still divided into two groups. Some leaders believed that the monarchy must remain as a steady influence, that reforms must begin within the government but without changing its shape. Liang Chi-chao, one of the two teachers who escaped from the Emperor's palace, and now a brilliant, witty, modern writer, was the leader of this group. Kang Yu-wei, the other teacher who escaped, agreed with him and was traveling about the world, trying, he said, to learn about the Western countries. He was head of the Pao Huang Huei, or Save the Emperor Society.

Liang Chi-chao was living in Japan at this time,

too. He and Sun Yat-sen had many talks together, never very satisfactory, perhaps, to either one. Liang was a product of the best classical Chinese education, and he had a subtle mind, both profound and lively. He was a true aristocrat, the heir of generations of educated people. Sun Yat-sen, on the other hand, was a man of the people, a product of missionary schools where he had received all too little of the classical Chinese tradition. He was practical and downright, a man of action, and he was convinced that the only hope for China was a complete change of the form of government.

Kang Yu-wei, also an intellectual aristocrat, believed with Liang Chi-chao that the common people of China were not ready for a democracy. "The Chinese people," he declared abroad, "are illiterate, uneducated, with no knowledge of national affairs. Democracy is a system of government for the educated."

But Sun Yat-sen thought better of his people. He believed that they would be able to govern themselves, once they were taught modern democratic techniques. As a matter of fact, they actually governed themselves very well already on the family and village level. They had only to be trained in provincial and national government. It was inevitable that Sun felt he had to separate himself from Liang Chi-chao and Kang Yu-wei and those whom they represented. "China is like the United States," he said. "Our provinces are like the states, and we need only a president to govern us all alike."

At the end of three years Sun Yat-sen decided it was time again to act. In February, 1904, war broke out between Japan and Russia. In March Sun Yat-sen left Honolulu for the American mainland. He knew now who his own people were. They were the plain people, the average Chinese, and he was determined to depend upon them. As he traveled, Kang Yu-wei was cultivating the higher Chinese and trying to influence Western opinion on the upper levels. When Sun Yat-sen reached an American city, he went immediately to the restaurant keepers, the laundrymen, and the little shopkeepers, and from there he added members to his Prosper China Society.

He had two keys which opened many doors to him. They were the old keys he had used in China. One was Christianity, and the other was the secret societies. The Chinese Christians and the missions in the Chinatowns were always his friends, and from them he could be sure of food and shelter. The secret societies, ignored by the wealthy and educated Chinese abroad, were nevertheless very strong in American cities, where the poorer Chinese had to help each other to live in a foreign country. The Americans knew the societies as "tongs," and seldom understood exactly what they were. Actually, they were the same old patriotic secret societies which through the centuries in

He was given a fine reception in Philadelphia

China were always dedicated to the return of Chinese self-government. Chinese alone in America naturally tended to find their brother members, whatever the society, and sometimes local enmities developed. Each group had its own secret language of signs. If a member entered a house with one foot over the doorsill and put an umbrella on the sill, it was a sign that he was a fugitive from the police and needed help. If when he drank his wine he held his wine bowl with a thumb and two fingers, it was a sign to others that he too was a brother. There was a big book of information on secret signs, whereby one Chinese could make known to another that he was a member of a brotherhood. The most important of the brotherhoods was The Chinese Patriotic Society, or I Hsing, to which about four-fifths of all the Chinese belonged. This was the society which Sun Yat-sen found waiting and ready to help him.

And how well they helped! "All over the world and especially in America," he said, "the legend has grown that the Chinese are selfish and mercenary. There never was a greater libel on a people. Many have given me their whole fortune. One Philadelphia laundryman called at my hotel after a meeting and thrusting a linen bag upon me went away without a word. It contained his entire savings for twenty years."

Quietly Sun Yat-sen moved from city to city, seeking his friends among ordinary folk. In New York he found his home with the pastor of the Chinese church, and in mission houses and laundries he gathered his audiences. Would these humble people benefit under the rule of a king or emperor? He could not believe it. They must trust only themselves. Theirs must be the government of which Lincoln dreamed, "a government of the people, by the people and for the people."

The year in America revived Sun Yat-sen's hopes and gave shape to his dreams. In the spring of 1905 he left for Europe to do his work there. Neither his coming nor his going was noticed.

The newspapers were already printing colorful stories of the dramatic arrival of the great Chinese reform leader, Kang Yu-wei, the teacher of the young Manchu Emperor of China. He was received by President Theodore Roosevelt in Washington and was given a splendid reception in Philadelphia by dignified and wealthy Chinese. Wearing a maroon-colored robe of brocaded satin he was escorted by two lines of young Chinese cadets in bright blue uniforms, carrying the dragon flag of Imperial Peking side by side with the Stars and Stripes while a hired band provided martial music. Thus Kang Yu-wei proceeded in state, accompanied by his military adviser, an American named Homer Lea, at his side.

A strange little figure, that military adviser, a twisted hunchback with burning eyes, a warped body encased in a fantastic uniform! But behind the burning eyes was a daring and imaginative brain.

7

The Hunchback

HOMER LEA WAS A LITTLE AMERICAN WITH A BIG dream. He had an agile and brilliant mind, but it had been shaped by the misfortune of his body. He longed to be big and he was small. He longed to be strong, and he was weak and almost never free from pain. He longed to be powerful and admired, and he feared he could be neither.

With all these longings, it was inevitable that Homer Lea's active and constantly revolving mind

should center early on militarism and the power
of weapons and war. By reading and study, he
became an expert in military subjects. His hero
was Napoleon, that hero of many men of small
stature. Because of his passionate interest in wars
and weapons and because he was born in California where there are many Chinese, Homer Lea
early became interested in the Chinese Revolution,
especially after the failure of the Boxer Rebellion.
When he was still a very young man he made a
trip to China, financed by San Francisco Chinese
as their agent. The trip was supposed to be a secret,
but he was so happy about it that he could not keep
it quiet. An article about him in a San Francisco
paper spoiled his mission, and although he went
anyway he could not accomplish anything. Back
in San Francisco again he organized the Reform
Cadets, a group of young Chinese who hoped to
go to China and form a modern army. Lea was
called General and he designed for himself a

gaudy uniform, put uniforms on the cadets and trained them daily in marching. When Kang Yu-wei came to America, he attached himself at once to this famous man.

Homer Lea was no fool, in spite of his oddities. It took only a little while for him to decide that the aristocratic scholar was not his man. He left Kang Yu-wei and went back to his cadets and considered what he should do next. Meantime he wrote a novel about China, a thriller. He kept on reading about China and Japan, and meditated his next book, not a novel, but a thriller of a different sort. It was to be entitled *The Valor of Ignorance*, and it would warn Americans that one day Japan would rise up to fight them.

Sun Yat-sen, meanwhile, had returned to China to make his third attempt at a revolution. He set up his headquarters in Canton. From there he directed the plot for a co-ordinated uprising over the country carried out by the secret societies and helped locally by students. With him were trusted Chinese friends whom he summoned from Honolulu. It was very difficult in so loose an organization to keep every move secret. Somehow or other the plot was discovered by government spies, and Sun Yat-sen and his Hawaiian friends had to leave on a moment's notice in small rowboats manned by Cantonese boat women. Out in the river they bribed the women to change garments with them, and in this disguise they escaped.

It was enough to discourage any man, and certainly Sun Yat-sen had his dark moments. His family was far away, he was seldom at home, and his children were growing up almost without his knowing them. What kept him from giving up? Only the daily sight of his countrymen—the hardworking, lowly and poor. They were everywhere about him, a fine honest industrious people, who had no chance for education or knowledge. Their children died in great numbers because there were

They left in rowboats manned by Cantonese boatwomen

almost no doctors. Even if they lived it was to
work incessantly for food and shelter. Cruel taxes
robbed them of most of their earnings. The courts
were unjust and did not protect them. In fact, the
Manchu government still did nothing for the people, and Sun Yat-sen felt more strongly than ever
that only a new government could make life better.

He would not give up. Three times his plans

had failed, but he would try again. This time he went to Manila to raise money. While he was there he met an American, Judge Linebarger, who was to be his friend and supporter for the rest of his life. Judge Linebarger wanted to meet Sun Yat-sen for a curious and personal reason. He had a Chinese cook whom he liked. One day the cook had come to him and asked for a month's leave. He confided that he had been sent for to help Sun Yat-sen. The judge gave the leave but the cook did not return for many months. When he did come back he was bone thin and scarred as from battle. But he was more enthusiastic than ever about the revolution, although his effort had failed, and he had been caught by government police, imprisoned, beaten and robbed of his possessions. Judge Linebarger was first indignant and then interested, and he determined that he must know Sun Yat-sen himself. From the day he met Sun in Manila he continued to be his friend.

When Sun had talked to the Chinese in Manila, he returned to his old base in Japan and there gave a lecture on some of his ideas, later to become his famous book, *The Three Principles of the People.* This lecture was so successful and so talked about that the Manchu government in Peking heard of it and insisted that Japan banish the rebel from their shores. This meant that Sun had now to find a new base.

He left the Japanese headquarters and its newspaper, *The Peoples' Paper*, in the hands of some of his young men. Taking two of his best men with him, he went to Annam in Indo-China and set up a new base in Hanoi. He gave up now the hope of help from Japan. Instead he sought the French, who, he felt, understood well the necessity for a revolution, because, like the Americans, they had had one of their own. He was the more hopeful, because when he was in Shanghai on his way to Annam, and aboard the ship which lay in the harbor at Woosung, a French general had called on him and offered help from France. He was glad to accept, and eight retired French army officers were actually placed in different parts of Central South China. They were to work with the Chinese revolutionists secretly and to bribe or influence the officers of the local provincial armies to desert and come over to Sun Yat-sen.

These efforts were so successful that very soon, too soon, alas, the revolutionaries held a large meeting in Wuchang, a midway city on the Yangtse River. In the audience was a general of the Imperial Army in disguise, who had been told of the meeting. Of course he reported all he heard to the Viceroy of the Province, who arrested and beheaded the Chinese leaders. The government sent a foreign spy to become friends with the old French officer in charge, who, trusting him, told him of the revolutionary plans. Upon this the

Manchu government sent protests to the French government in Paris, but received no reply.

Meanwhile Sun Yat-sen, always dauntless, was in Annam organizing men and buying munitions again from Japan. He was helped by French officers, and this time he laid his plans very carefully indeed, taking more than a year to perfect them. Guns and ammunition were to be sent from the group in Japan. His friend, Huang Hsing, was the vice-president of the whole movement. He had taken a military course in Japan and came to help organize an army. The revolutionary soldiers were stimulated and inspired until their morale was so high that they called themselves Dare-to-Dies.

Sun Yat-sen watched for his chance at a fourth try. It came soon. Just over the French border in China a rebellion against high taxes broke out, and the Manchu government sent two generals and some thousands of soldiers to quell it. Sun Yat-sen sent some of his men across to talk with the generals and soldiers and persuade them to help in the revolution. He sent other men to persuade the peasants and country people to help when the moment came for attack.

His hopes were high. He believed that now his troops could march swiftly enough, gathering discontented soldiers and people as they went, so that in a short time half of China would be in open revolt against the Manchus. Alas, he seemed doomed to failure by his own men! The guns and ammunition from Japan did not arrive in time at the proper place, and therefore the generals and soldiers sent by the Manchus prudently did not revolt. Sun's men, left alone, had to retreat. Sun, in despair, organized a second invasion, which he led himself, but the Imperial soldiers defeated him and he had to retreat again. This time the Manchu government insisted that the French government banish Sun Yat-sen. Again he had to change his base, leaving only subordinates to hold what they could. Sun went to Singapore.

Meanwhile Huang made another invasion over the border, and with only about two hundred soldiers he was able to maintain his position in that rough countryside for two months or so. When his ammunition gave out, he returned to Yunnan.

Another attempt was made on the border by a sympathizer with little military training, and Sun Yat-sen sent Huang Hsing and his men to help him. The attempt failed, for the French would not allow Huang Hsing to cross the border. He returned to Annam, having collected more than five hundred discontented men for his army meanwhile. The result of this was that the French deported all the revolutionaries to Singapore, and banished the leaders. At Singapore the English did not want them, but finally they were allowed to land. They scattered over the country, sowing everywhere the seeds of discontent.

Four more quick defeats had now to be added to the list of Sun's failures. A lesser man would have given up and gone back to quiet family life. In this man, however, each failure only seemed to create more determination. The French government of Annam resolutely banished not only Sun Yat-sen but six hundred other revolutionaries. They were all piled on one ship and sent to Singapore, where the English, who controlled that city, did not want to receive them. Since they had nowhere to go they were finally allowed to land, and they spread among the people, jobless discontented men, to foment other discontented groups and recruit new members for their party. From here two attacks were organized in an effort to capture the great and rich city of Canton. Both failed, and in the last attempt Sun Yat-sen lost seventy-two of his finest and most devoted young men.

Ten failures, and the last one so costly! He had

Attacks were organized against the city of Canton

to go to America again and find money for the next trial. But he needed more than money. He needed advice, and where would he get that?

One night after a revolutionary meeting in Chinatown in a great American city, a little hunchback with a long pale face came up to him.

"I should like to throw in my lot with you," he said. "I should like to help you. I believe your propaganda will succeed."

"Thank you," Sun Yat-sen replied. He was not impressed with the small tragic figure, and later he asked a friend who the little hunchback was.

"That is General Homer Lea," the man replied. "He is perhaps the most brilliant military genius now alive. He is a master of modern warfare and the author of a first-rate book."

"He has offered to throw in his lot with me!" Sun Yat-sen exclaimed.

The next day he went early to call upon Homer Lea. The more he talked with the strange little man the more impressed he was.

"When I am President of China," he declared, "I will make you my chief military adviser."

"Do not wait until you are President of China," Homer Lea replied. "You may want me before then."

It was new inspiration for Sun Yat-sen, and he needed it. He was living in a cheap hotel in a bare and wretched little room. He had a few clothes, a few books and nothing else. A price of five hundred thousand dollars was on his head, but he had no guards to protect him as he came and went. Yet he was not discouraged. When an American friend told him that he should not be alone, lest he be killed, he replied tranquilly:

"If they had killed me some years ago, it would have been a pity for the cause. I was indispensable then. Now my life does not matter. Our organization is complete. There are plenty of Chinese to take my place. It does not matter now if they kill me."

8

The Outbreak

TEN FAILURES, SUN YAT-SEN HAD COUNTED, AND there must have been many lonely nights when he pondered over them and wondered if he could ever succeed. What he did not know was that these failures, made in different parts of his country by young Chinese from all over the world, were not failures. They had touched the hearts of many Chinese people, lighting hope everywhere for a government of their own. They could take their beloved country back again from the foreign Manchu rulers; they could build roads and schools and railways; they could build ships and factories and give men work so that the children could have a chance for a better life. They knew now that the world around them was changing and that they must change, too. The old sleeping China, the giant of four thousand years, must wake and be-

The young Emperor was killed by servants of the Empress

come a new China ready to take her place in the new world.

Even the old Empress Dowager knew it in Peking, and unwillingly she allowed her ministers to make more reforms. She did not really change, however, and of the three men she declared she would never forgive Sun Yat-sen was one. The other two were Liang Chi-chao and Kang Yu-wei, the young Emperor's two tutors who had escaped her. She never forgave the young Emperor, either. He was still a prisoner in his palace. And when in 1908 the old Empress knew she was about to die of illness and age, she kept herself alive by sheer will power until her servants had poisoned the young Emperor. Then she died. The heir to the throne was a baby prince, and his young and gentle mother became the Empress. A regent was appointed, but nobody took the new regime seriously, for the people felt a great change was near. The dynasty was dying.

All this was happening while Sun Yat-sen was traveling in America, trying to collect more money from the Chinese there, and talking with Homer Lea about building an army. Homer Lea told him that he must not try to fight with untrained men. He could not succeed and the men would be sacrificed. Sun must, Homer Lea said, build a real military academy, for the training of soldiers of the revolutionary army. It sounded impossible. Where would Sun Yat-sen get money enough to build a military academy to train soldiers? Nevertheless he listened to the little American, learning all that he could of military science, remembering it for the future.

One day in the fall of 1911 while he was traveling in a western state, Sun received a cablegram from Hankow. He could not read it because it was in code. He had packed his code book in his trunk and sent it ahead to Denver, Colorado, where he planned to stay for a few days. When he reached there he read the telegram. It said, "We Wuchang revolutionists are ready to attack. Send money."

Money? He had none. He was tired and he decided he would wait until morning to think the matter out. Morning came and he rose early as usual. He left his cheap hotel room to find a restaurant where he could get breakfast for as little money as possible. On the way he bought a newspaper and while he walked he unfolded it and saw the headlines. He was stunned.

"Wuchang Occupied by Revolutionists!" These were the words that flashed before his eyes. Those hot-headed brave young men had not waited. They had not waited for money from him or even for guidance. They had gathered themselves together and attacked the Viceroy of Kiangsi Province in his palace and had sent him running. Then they had occupied the city. This tremendous news was compressed in a few lines, all too short, but there

Sun Yat-sen realized that no one in the car knew him

it was. Ought he to go back? But he had no money to take with him. He decided to go to New York, where there were the most Chinese, and beg them to help. He bought a ticket for a day coach to the East, and when the train stopped in St. Louis he rushed out to buy another newspaper. There was still more exciting news. The revolutionists, the paper said, were setting up a republican form of government, based on the American pattern, and Sun Yat-sen was to be the first President!

He went back to the dusty red plush seat in the crowded car and read the paper again and again. No one knew him. He was a stranger among strangers, but his young countrymen called him their President. They were overthrowing a foreign government and setting up in its place a government like the American government, a people's government. Though no one in the coach dreamed of such a thing, he was the President of a country far older and more vast than the United States.

Of course his heart was hot with joy and pride. Of course he was humble and proud together, humble because he was a man of natural humility and proud because after all the failures, and quite without his help, strong young men had carried out his dream. He was too practical, however, to think of the dream as fulfilled. Only the first step had been taken, in one city in one province in China. It was a toehold in a mighty empire. It was only a beginning.

How could he help those brave young men? Besides money they needed friends. Most of all, they needed recognition from other governments. What government could be friendly to a young government, a newborn babe of a government among others old and established? The American people, he felt sure, were friendly enough. They had once had the same experience. They, too, had rebelled against a dominating government from abroad and they, too, had set up a new young weak government which had become strong and powerful because the people made it. That was all he wanted for his own country, a government which, created by the people, would work for the welfare of the people as the old selfish Manchu government had never done. The people's money, the taxes, had gone mainly to enrich the rulers and not to help the people.

Americans, Sun Yat-sen told himself, he could count upon. The French people he believed would be friendly, too, since they also had overthrown selfish rulers and the battle cry of their revolution had been Liberty, Equality and Fraternity. But Germany and Russia were friendly to the Manchu government, and he could not count on their help. In Japan the people were friendly to him, but the government was not. Then he remembered that recently an alliance had been made between the British government and the Japanese government. England was much more powerful than Japan.

If he could win the approval of the British government, then perhaps England could influence
Japan. To England therefore he would go.

His Chinese friends in New York helped him
to get quietly on a ship bound for England. When
he reached London he hoped to be able to remain
unknown until he had met with some responsible
persons in the British government. His old friends,
Dr. and Mrs. Cantlie, expected him any day. In
spite of misfortunes, strange luck followed Sun
Yat-sen. He delayed a few hours in going to see
the Cantlies and meanwhile the Chinese Embassy
received a cablegram addressed to him. They did
not know where he was and they sent the cablegram by messenger to the Cantlie house. Mrs.
Cantlie could say very truthfully that Sun Yat-sen
was not there, but the messenger had been gone
only an hour or two when the doorbell rang and
Sun Yat-sen appeared. Mrs. Cantlie had made a
copy of the coded cablegram. She greeted Sun and

handed it to him. It was the formal invitation from the young revolutionary party in China to come back and be the President of the new Chinese Republic. Now he knew that he was really wanted. His chance had come to serve his country.

But he could not go home at once. He must make sure that the British government would be friendly to his new government.

A group of bankers from Western nations, called the Consortium, had for some years been making loans to the Manchu government to help build railways in China. Very few railroads were built, but now another loan was about to be made. Sun Yat-sen called upon the Consortium and boldly asked that the loan be made instead to the new government of the Republic of China. The Consortium replied that if and when other governments recognized the new government, they would so make the loan.

Then Sun Yat-sen asked for still more. He asked that he be allowed to enter freely the British colonial ports of Singapore and Hongkong. That permission was given, and in great joy he made ready to hasten back to his own country. At last he had success enough to work with, and he wanted to use it quickly.

Again he profited from a coincidence. Homer Lea, who had been very ill, was in Europe for his health. Now he was better. He told Yat-sen that he wanted to go to China as his military adviser and help him to organize a good army. Sun Yat-sen agreed, and after a friendly meeting with Clemenceau in Paris, he took ship at Marseilles. On the ship he found Homer Lea, bright with enthusiasm and rich with plans. The little hunchback was a born lover of publicity and he determined to keep Sun Yat-sen before the world. Of course he himself would be there, too, close at Sun's side.

Together then the two friends crossed the sea. At Singapore a mighty crowd waited for Sun on the dock and a wealthy Chinese took him off to spend the night at his home. But Sun Yat-sen did not delay his journey. He was dreaming of his own country. For sixteen years he had been a fugitive, creeping silently and secretly over the borders. Now he was coming back in triumph, the chosen President of a new regime. He knew very well that he had far to go. The long struggle to establish the Republic lay ahead. He could not rest but he was not afraid of struggle. His whole life had been struggle.

On a cool winter day, the twenty-first of December, he reached Hongkong. There he was met by one of his best men, Hu Han-min. They went on to Shanghai at once and reached there on Christmas Day. The Revolutionists had set up a National Assembly which had met earlier, and on December the twenty-ninth the Assembly formally elected Sun Yat-sen President. On New Year's day, 1912, in Nanking, he took the oath of office.

9

A Nation United

NANKING WAS AN OLD WALLED CITY WHERE ONCE
the Ming Emperors, the last Chinese dynasty, had
lived and ruled. Outside the curving walls stone
paved roads led through farm villages and fields
to the foot of Purple Mountain where the Ming
Emperors were buried. But inside the city Sun
Yat-sen proudly announced the new government
which from now on would be under the leadership of presidents chosen by the people, and not
under the control of emperors.

At the same time he changed the calendar. China has always reckoned time by the moon. Now, Sun Yat-sen decided, she was to reckon time by the sun, as the Western peoples did. All the old feast days, which the Chinese people had enjoyed for centuries, would be upset, but Sun did not care. Perhaps he did not care enough. Perhaps he had been lonely too long, and far away from the life of his own people.

At any rate, the day which declared such a triumph was followed by many troubles. Over the southern half of the country the Manchus were in flight. Many were murdered by angry Chinese who were enraged by years of oppression. Delicate ladies, reared as princesses in the Manchu sections of great cities, had to run for their lives into the hills and valleys. They hid in holes and behind the graves that cover many Chinese hillsides, and relentlessly the revengeful people pursued them and murdered them. Against such anger Sun Yat-sen was helpless. It was the people's turn now. He could not control them. Fifteen of the eighteen provinces of China joined the new government, but the three northern provinces held out against Sun Yat-sen. Yuan Shih-kai was still Premier of the Manchu government.

Sun Yat-sen could not be happy until the whole country was united in one Republic. He had studied thoroughly the French Revolution of a century before. Like the Chinese, the French had rebelled against their selfish rulers. Men and women had worked together to overthrow a corrupt king and his court and they had dreamed of a good government that would help the people honestly. Yet the ordinary people were not able to make such a government when the king was gone. They were men and women who had been busy in fields and little shops, and they did not understand how to run a whole country. Bad men got into power and the result of the French Revo-

Many ran for their lives into the hills and valleys

lution for a long time was only more confusion and unhappiness for the people than they had had before.

Sun Yat-sen did not want this to be so in his country. He knew that the Chinese people did not know how to make a government, either, and he had planned three steps, each to last for several years, while the people learned how to build a real Republic.

First, he planned, he would set up a military government until the whole of China was under its control, even if he had to fight Yuan Shih-kai for the three northern provinces. Next, he would let the people govern themselves in the villages and the towns, and when they understood how to do this he would let them govern their provinces. When most of the provinces had their own government, they would make a constitution, like the American constitution, which could set up a central government for the nation. In this way, he thought, the Chinese could avoid the mistakes that the French people had made.

But China was neither France nor the United States. It was far older and more vast than those countries, the people many times greater in number and their ways of life much more deeply established. It was not as easy to change the government of a great and old nation as it was to change thirteen little new colonies or even a small old nation in Europe.

Troubles began to cluster again about Sun Yat-sen like crows in a corn field. First of all, Homer Lea died before he could help to make an army. Then Yuan Shih-kai, the Chinese Premier of the Manchu Emperor, still in Peking and in control of the North, would not accept the Republic in the South under Sun Yat-sen. Sun Yat-sen, the Imperial government said, was a Cantonese, and northern people did not like the people of Canton. Morever, they said, Sun Yat-sen was a rebel and a revolutionist and he had no experience as a president or in making a government. There was some truth in this, yet the revolutionists were not willing to yield. They had dreamed of making all China into one great Republic and getting rid, forever, of the Manchus.

Neither side would yield, and it looked as if a civil war would break out. If it did, could Sun Yat-sen win? The Manchu government had a large army and he did not. They had old power and he did not. Poor as they were, their resources were much greater than his. Prudent friends advised Sun to make some sort of compromise in order to avoid war. Why not suggest that if the young Emperor, under the Regency, would abdicate, then he, Sun Yat-sen, would resign from his place as President? Each side would gain as well as lose. There would be no more Emperors, the Republic could be saved and another President could be chosen, someone both sides could accept.

Sun Yat-sen was proud. He would not demand position for his own sake. Whatever was best for the people, he said, was what he would do.

When Yuan Shih-kai, the Premier, heard this, he at once advised the little Empress that the time had come for her to abdicate with her son, the baby Emperor. If she did so, he promised that she and the other members of the Imperial family would be treated well so long as they lived. Then he sent a telegram to Sun Yat-sen in Nanking say-

ing, "A Republic is the best form of government.
. . . Henceforth, forever, we shall not allow a
monarchical government in our country."

There was nothing now for Sun Yat-sen to do
except to resign. He had been President for only
a few weeks, but by resigning he could save his
country from a civil war. Perhaps this was, after
all, the way in which he could best serve his people. With a sad heart and a stern will he sent in his
resignation. On February thirteenth he wrote to
the Nanking Council, which he himself had set up,
"Today I present you my resignation and request
you to elect a good and talented man as the new
President."

What man? There was only one to which
the North would agree. He was Yuan Shih-kai.
After all, it was said, he had ended the Manchu
throne and he deserved a reward. Then, too, he
had long experience in government and he had
never been a rebel or a revolutionist.

The ceremony was a magnificent one

The three northern provinces agreed to join the Republic under Yuan as President. The nation was unified at last! The old imperial flag with its yellow dragon was cast aside and a new flag was made, the flag of the Republic of China. It was made of five wide bars, each standing for one great group of the Chinese people. The red bar at the top stood for the peoples under the old Empire. The yellow bar next stood for the people of Manchuria. The bar of blue beneath stood for the people of Mongolia, the white for the Tibetans and the black for the Mohammedans. Thus the five groups who had lived under the rule for centuries of the Chinese Empire, were now one under the Republic.

Even Sun Yat-sen began to hope that his sacrifice had been worth making. He was an unselfish and honest man, and he liked to believe that all men were good. He had to be hopeful, and he was hopeful on that day of the great celebration in

Nanking, the day after Yuan Shih-kai was elected President. The ceremony was a magnificent one. A mighty procession led by Sun Yat-sen walked between the granite figures of animals that form a wide avenue to the Ming Tombs. Up that avenue Sun Yat-sen walked with the cabinet and his officials and soldiers. Then before the tomb of the first Ming Emperor, who had been a revolutionist, too, in his time, Sun Yat-sen took his stand. A hundred years before Columbus had set out to find India and had instead landed upon the vast continent which was to be America, that old Ming Emperor had been buried in the flank of Purple Mountain. To his spirit Sun Yat-sen, following the ancient Chinese custom, made a long and eloquent speech, describing the revolution and announcing the Republic.

At the end he cried to the dead Emperor, "Your Majesty! Your people have come here today to inform Your Majesty of the final victory. May this lofty shrine wherein you rest gain fresh luster from today's event and may your example inspire your descendants in the times which are to come. Spirit, accept this offering!"

Now, Sun Yat-sen thought, he was really free to work for his people. He wanted the new President to keep the capital of the Republic at Nanking, the ancient home of the Ming Emperors, who were Chinese. But President Yuan decided to stay in Peking, the old Manchu capital, where he had the support of his troops.

Still Sun Yat-sen was hopeful.

"We have an enormous amount of work ahead of us," he declared with all his old energy and with new hope, "and we must accomplish it in order that China may rank as a great power among the family of nations."

He planned to return to his home city of Canton and begin there by changing it into a new modern city.

134

He was not allowed to do so. All over China people wanted to see him and hear him. What they saw was a man in Western clothes, his black hair cut short in the American fashion. He held his head high, he had dark honest eyes that looked straight ahead, a calm face, a small moustache. What they heard was an earnest voice speaking urgent and eloquent words of faith in the goodness of the Chinese people and hope for their future. No wonder he was popular. Everywhere he went people crowded to hear him. He spoke in schools to students, in churches to Christians, in halls to all who came. He spoke quietly in a clear voice, without gestures or show, but what he said was so powerful that people listened sometimes for three or four hours at a stretch. What he talked about was always for the good of the people. He told them what they must do in order to make China strong and prosperous. He spoke about the people's livelihood, about patriotism, about good government for all. His purpose was to teach his people how to make their country modern and strong.

In Peking President Yuan Shih-kai felt that he, too, must honor the man whom all were honoring, and he invited Sun Yat-sen to come and visit him. It was summer, the time when Peking is most beautiful. The sky was nearly always clear, and the sun shone down upon the blue-tiled roofs of the Temple of Heaven, and upon the yellow tiles of the old palace roofs. Sun Yat-sen decided to accept President Yuan's invitation, although some of his best friends thought it would be better if he did not. Strange rumors were beginning to be whispered about President Yuan. It was said that he really wanted to be the Emperor. Two revolutionary heroes who had been visiting in Peking had been killed without trial. This ought not to happen in the Republic, Sun's friends agreed. Was Yuan Shih-kai plotting something?

Sun Yat-sen was afraid of nothing, as usual, and so he went on to Peking. It was August, and the mountains outside the city walls were as blue as the temple roofs. President Yuan received Sun with great honor, and he was given handsome rooms for his stay. The retired Empress sent her greetings and the Manchu princes, no longer rulers, gave him a great feast. Sun Yat-sen spoke in one of the big churches and it was crowded. Best of all, President Yuan, always wearing his long Chinese robes, spent much time with Sun, listening to his ideas. Sun told him that railroads must be built above all else. He wanted to see China covered with a network of good railways, so that travel and trade could grow. President Yuan seemed to agree with everything, and he asked Sun Yat-sen to take charge of this development, giving him power to make plans for borrowing money from foreign countries to build the railroads.

Sun Yat-sen stayed for more than a month, believing that President Yuan was a good and strong man who wanted to do his best for the Chinese people. Then, saying good-by, he went away to work happily on his dream of the railroads that were to tie together the huge spreading country of eighteen provinces. He decided first to go to Japan to study the railroads there and to discuss loans from the Japanese government.

Money was always Sun's difficulty and now more than ever. The new government had no money to begin to make improvements, and money had to be borrowed from other nations. Yet none would lend money without hope of getting it back again and so security had to be given. The Western nations who made the Consortium were willing to lend money to the new Chinese government only on very hard terms. They said they wanted all the taxes on salt. Everybody had to buy salt and, since this was one of the biggest sources of money for the new government, the Chinese people were angry, and especially angry when the Consortium said they did not trust the Chinese but must collect the tax themselves. President Yuan went on taking money from the Consortium meanwhile, and good Chinese were fearful lest the Western nations would demand payment in ways that would rob China of her independence. The United States government sympathized with the Chinese and withdrew from the Consortium. In spite of all this, President Yuan insisted on the loans.

Suddenly a dreadful thing happened. Sung Chiao-jen was the head of Sun Yat-sen's Nationalist party, or the Kuomintang, as it was called in Chinese. He was a man who had been earnest in opposing the taking of money from foreign nations at such high price. Suddenly this man was murdered just as he was about to get on the train at Shanghai to go to Peking. Everybody was shocked. Sung had long been a friend and supporter of Sun Yat-sen's and this murder could not have taken place unless it had been ordered by President Yuan.

No one now could control President Yuan. Even Sun Yat-sen saw how mistaken he had been about this man. He cabled to the Consortium then meeting in London, and begged them not to give money to Yuan. The Chinese people, he said, were so angry that the government could not go on as it was. The Consortium paid no attention to the cable. The five nations saw their chance to get power in China, and they made huge loans at once to President Yuan.

Sun Yat-sen called upon Yuan Shih-kai to resign. Yuan would not. The followers of Sun Yat-sen decided to fight. An attack was made on a garrison in Kiukiang, a city in a middle province, and Huang Hsing went to Nanking, which declared independence of Peking and President Yuan. Four provinces joined the revolt. But Yuan Shih-kai gathered his armies and routed the rebels, and established himself with magnificent ceremony as President for a five-year term. Sun Yat-sen again fled to Japan for three years.

Troubles were not over for Yuan Shih-kai, either. Sun Yat-sen had taught his people well. They did not intend to give up the struggle for a really democratic government, and they believed that Yuan Shih-kai did not know how to make such a government. He was too skilled in old imperialistic ways. But time had to tell the full story. Meanwhile, Sun Yat-sen continued in exile.

10

Civil Wars

THE YEARS THAT NOW FOLLOWED WERE THE
darkest that Sun Yat-sen had yet known. He had
believed that the task of his life was successfully
accomplished, and his country united under one
flag and one democratic government. Now he saw
that there was neither unity nor democratic government, and he himself was exiled in Japan, while
greedy power groups tried to get as much as they
could of China's resources. Most of all, Sun Yat-

sen blamed the foreign bankers who lent money to Yuan Shih-kai.

"Not our own people, not our own mistakes, drove us from China," he declared, "but foreign money, deliberately employed for the break-up of our country. The foreign bankers of the five-power group held the balance of power between the North and the South for three years. When we were in power they starved us of the credit, except on the most humiliating terms. . . . Last year's personal loan of five million dollars to Yuan Shih-kai, fought to the last ditch by every constitutional power in China, simply put a club in the hands of the North with which they straightway smashed our cause. That huge bribe, and that alone, is the reason we are here today."

There was some truth in this accusation, although one can suppose that it would be hard for Sun Yat-sen, the dangerous revolutionist, to see himself as being unworthy of credit from large established financial interests. On the other hand, these interests knew Yuan Shih-kai from previous experience with the old Imperial government, and they felt that they could rely on him.

The real truth, however, was that Sun Yat-sen, while he was and will forever be an inspiration to his people, was nevertheless not a good organizer. He knew how to make people think and feel. He could stir them to angers and hopes. He could make them long for liberty and a better life. He could persuade them to action. But like so many other revolutionary leaders, once the revolution was over, he could not set up a sound and workable government. He could tell people what they needed, but he could not bring it to pass. He could overthrow, but he could not build up. Time and again he had failed even during the revolution because his attacks were badly planned and ill-timed. At the very hour when the people most needed a leader and organizer, he failed them. Good man though he was, he really did not know how to make the government of which he dreamed and which he longed to give to his people. Yuan Shih-kai was not such a good man, nor did he have the interests of the people so deeply at heart as did Sun Yat-sen. Yet he was able to organize a sort of government, even if it was not the one so hoped for. Some sort of success might have come slowly to the Chinese Republic had Yuan not made a private plan of his own, later, to do away with the Republic altogether and set up the Empire again in the old tradition with himself as the First Emperor of a new Chinese dynasty.

Meanwhile, Sun Yat-sen might have been in complete despair had not someone come into his life during these years to give him hope again. He had always been a lonely man, perhaps one of the loneliest men who ever lived. Men who dream big dreams and give up their lives for their dreams are nearly always lonely. They cannot stay at home and enjoy their families, and sometimes their families do not even want them at home. So it had been with Sun Yat-sen.

His parents had blamed him for being a rebel and though the wife they had chosen for him was a good woman, yet she had never liked to travel with him and be a part of his life. She had been educated in the old-fashioned Chinese idea that the son's wife belongs to the family and must take care of his parents and this she had done faithfully. Sun Yat-sen scarcely knew his own children, so constantly had he been away from home. His brother, Ah-mei, though he was often kind, had never understood him. Now some of his best friends, too, had been killed by Yuan Shih-kai. He had to begin over again, and begin alone to rebuild the Republic.

Perhaps he might not have had the heart to try except that he fell in love for the first time in his life. His old friend, Charley Soong, the merchant in Shanghai, was now a very rich and successful one. Mr. Soong was a Methodist Christian, and his wife was a good Methodist, too. They had six children, all of whom Mr. Soong had sent to America to be educated, because he believed very much in American ways. Of these six children three were girls, and the eldest girl, Ai-lien, was Sun Yat-sen's secretary. There was no need for any of the girls to work, but they had caught from their father his belief in Sun Yat-sen and his faith in the American form of government and American ways. So Ai-lien, when she came back from college in America, wanted to work for Sun Yat-sen. Now, however, she was ready to give up her job because she had decided to marry a young man named H. H. Kung. She wanted to find someone to take her place, someone who could be trusted and who could understand Sun Yat-sen. She thought of her second sister who was just graduating from college in America. This was her sister

Ching-ling, a beautiful shy graceful girl. Ching-ling had always been a warm-hearted believer in the revolution. When the Republic was declared, she had written a school essay about it, although she was in America. "The Revolution has established liberty and equality in China," she said.

Yes, Ching-ling was the one to take her place, the elder sister decided.

As for Sun Yat-sen, he had never seen anyone like Soong Ching-ling. She was young, she was beautiful, she was intelligent. She knew English and French as well as her own language, and she had followed every step of his life and work. She knew and sympathized with his problems and was ready to help and encourage him. These two people, so well suited to each other, the man so lonely and the woman so able to be his companion and friend, soon loved each other.

Yet even this love, happy as it was to prove, had deep difficulties for Sun Yat-sen. His wife had been a faithful and good woman, by all standards. She had borne him two daughters and a son, and she had cared for his old parents until they died. When she was able, she had even tried to make a home for Sun Yat-sen himself. She had gone to Nanking when he was President, and had presided over his house there. Sun Yat-sen appreciated her good qualities and he had never blamed her for her lack of education, especially as she had learned to read, for his sake.

In spite of the cordial relationship between them, the sad truth nevertheless was that there could be no real companionship, and Sun Yat-sen had remained a lonely man. His brother, Ah-mei, had become the head of the Sun clan after their old father's death. He had taken care of Mrs. Sun and the three children, while Sun Yat-sen devoted himself to his cause. The children were sent to America to be educated, and this had still further separated the family. In 1913 the elder daughter,

Annie, died, after she had finished college and had come back to join her mother. Thereafter Sun Yat-sen kept his son, Sun Fo, with him as he came and went, and the younger daughter lived with her mother.

Sun Yat-sen was deeply troubled as he considered what he ought to do now. He longed for the companionship of Ching-ling, and yet he did not wish to hurt the good woman who was the mother of his children. She had given him no cause for divorce, according to Chinese law, and she freely granted her consent to his taking another wife who could go with him in his travels as she could not. This was according to Chinese custom and did not mean that she would be displaced in the family. But Ching-ling, young and modern, did not wish to be a secondary wife. It was a predicament, for this was a time of transition between old ways and new, and there was no real solution to the problem. Sun Yat-sen could only make the best of it.

He accepted gratefully his first wife's consent to his marriage to Soong Ching-ling, and at last the ceremony took place quietly in Japan.

They were married in that most difficult and confused year of 1915 when there was no real government left in China and when war was raging in Europe. In the midst of all that was despairing and troublesome, Sun Yat-sen had for the first time a home and a companion, and he faced the future without fear. Beside him stood Ching-ling, able and ready to help him. Thereafter he separated himself entirely from his first wife except to see that she lived in comfort, and Ching-ling became his real wife.

He needed this strong true young wife, for the next years were to be the hardest of his life. While Yuan Shih-kai was getting loans from foreign bankers, Sun Yat-sen was trying to get loans from the Japanese government in order to overthrow Yuan Shih-kai. He set up a new revolutionary

party, the Kemingtang, rejecting the old Nationalist party, or Kuomintang, which had been his
former party, and he promised the Japanese large
benefits later in China if they would help him now
in his plans.

In 1914 the First World War had broken out,
and Japanese ambitions soared. Now they could
begin to establish a vast empire in China. They
could make use of the split between Sun Yat-sen
and Yuan Shih-kai, and by helping to overthrow
Yuan Shih-kai, they would put Sun Yat-sen under
great obligation so that when he got back to his
country again, he would be compelled to give
Japan first place among all foreign powers. China
would then be their sphere of influence.

Meanwhile, Yuan, without knowing it, helped
to bring about his own downfall. After the Second
Revolution, as it was called, when Sun Yat-sen
had been compelled to leave China, Yuan Shih-kai
had got rid of all those who had helped Sun. Any

man who had been interested in setting up the Republic of China found himself without a job, and one of Yuan's men took his place. Yuan Shih-kai took more and more power into his own hands, and the ideal of the Republic began to fade away, or so it seemed. But Yuan Shih-kai went too far and too quickly. In the winter of 1914, while Sun was plotting desperately with the Japanese, President Yuan revived the old Imperial New Year's ceremonies at the Temple of Heaven in Peking, and he himself took the part which in the past had been performed only by an emperor. There had been many rumors that he wanted to set up a dynasty and climb on the Imperial throne, but here was proof. Rumblings were heard all over China.

By August, 1915, the danger was clear and people were growing angry. Sun Yat-sen with all his failures had planted deep in the hearts of his countrymen the hope of a republican government. They did not want the old monarchy back, and they did not trust Yuan Shih-kai as a ruler. Yet Yuan himself did not see the signs. He pretended that he must yield to advice and he announced that the new dynasty would start on January the first, 1916, with himself as its First Emperor.

The revolt was swift. Not Sun Yat-sen this time, who was still in Japan, but Liang Chi-chao led the new rebellion. He fled to Yunnan, a province in the far south, and there with the help of a general who had been his pupil, he began the rebellion against Yuan Shih-kai. Yunnan seceded from Yuan's control, and six other provinces followed. The country was split, and the people in full revolution again—the Third Revolution as it was called. So serious did the situation become that even Yuan Shih-kai saw that he had made a mistake. At last advice from abroad as well as at home compelled him to withdraw, a broken-hearted and humiliated man, and six months later he died. The Vice-President became temporary President.

Now Sun Yat-sen could come home. He was hopeful again and enthusiastic, and as soon as he reached Shanghai he made a long speech on "The Republican Form of Government." But he did not want to be President. Perhaps he knew now his own weaknesses. He wanted instead to devote himself to the education of his people in how to make and keep a Republic.

President Li, however, was in difficulties. The American government wished China to enter the World War on the Allied side. President Li did not want a war, nor did Sun Yat-sen, but the Premier, Tuan Chi-jui, wanted to join the World War. He felt this would bring China benefits from the Western nations. Since the matter could not be decided, the generals, who were actually the provincial or regional war lords, were called to Peking to give their advice. Of course, being professional soldiers, they wanted war and war was decided upon. Immediately the generals, feeling their power, began to speak against the new constitution then being made. When Dr. C. T. Wang, the Chairman of the Committee for Drafting the New Constitution, made a speech about the favorable aspects of the document, the northern war lords declared themselves independent altogether of the Republic and withdrew to their provinces.

Sun Yat-sen, of course, was with the constitutionalists, but power was with the war lords. He could only protest, and when republican officials fled from Peking to Shanghai he declared he would retire with them to Canton and set up a really constitutional Republic, even though it divided China. It was the beginning of his long and fresh struggle to keep alive on Chinese soil the National Republic of China.

The country was now divided between the Southern Republic and the war lords who were the rulers in the provinces. How were the people ever to be gathered together again under one flag?

Any other nation would have been destroyed by such civil wars. But the Chinese people are old and their country is vast. While wars were fought in one place and another between the different war lords, yet the good common people in villages and towns and cities went on living decently and working hard. They were civilized people and they had through the centuries learned that if people live decently and work hard and respect each other, then it is quite possible to live for a while without a government and even without police. Policemen, after all, are needed only to protect people from each other, and if there is mutual respect and good behavior people can manage themselves. The Chinese had long ago learned this lesson.

Sun Yat-sen knew the goodness of his people, and this time he decided that he would let them live in their own way until he had time to teach them how to make an efficient national government for themselves. Yuan Shih-kai had been experienced only in the old-fashioned Imperial government, and perhaps it was natural for him to try to set up that government again. But the people had decided against Yuan, and now they needed only to be taught how to make a government for themselves.

In the midst of the civil war Sun Yat-sen began to write a book, *The Three Principles of the People*. In this book he wanted to tell his people exactly what they must do in order that China could be a real and strong Republic. "To know is easy but to do is hard." This was the old Chinese proverb, and Sun Yat-sen hated it more than ever. He thought people still quoted it to excuse themselves from doing anything because action is hard. "The idea that action is difficult is my enemy," he wrote. "To say that knowing is easy while acting is hard is an enemy worse than all the Manchu emperors, for the Manchus could only kill our bodies, but this idea can kill our wills and our souls.

When we truly believe that a plan can be acted upon, we can do it. But when we do not believe, we do nothing and all our plans are useless. Every day my heart aches because we do nothing."

While he was writing down his teachings of action, the northern war lords continued their fighting against the South. Although the World War ended at last, it seemed as if Sun Yat-sen's dream of a Republic united under the one five-barred flag would never come true. The northern war lords did not want Sun Yat-sen, and so he continued with the South, although not always as President, for he preferred not to take that post. He lived in between times in Shanghai, and still he hoped that somehow his side would win. He tried, too, to make Canton a modern city, appointing his son, Sun Fo, who had been educated in America, as the mayor. Meanwhile, in Peking, a northern war lord, Wu Pei-fu, had set up Li Yuan-hung again as a puppet President.

Sun Yat-sen decided finally to attack the North, with the help of a young southern war lord, Chen Chiung-ming. Hope was natural to him, and perhaps it was his strength. At least it kept him from giving up. This time he had also the help of a young soldier, Chiang Kai-shek. But he counted very much upon General Chen, a handsome and highly educated young man. Alas, before the attack could be made, news came that the handsome General Chen had betrayed him. Instead of helping Sun Yat-sen, he decided to attack Canton and take it for himself. Chiang Kai-shek had warned Sun Yat-sen that General Chen could not be trusted, but Sun had not heeded the warning. Chiang was right.

Suddenly one early June morning before dawn the battle began. Sun Yat-sen was aroused from his sleep in the presidential palace and hurried away to a ship waiting in harbor. His life must not be risked or the South would have no leader.

They saved themselves by pretending to be dead

Madame Sun felt that she would be in no danger, and although Sun was anxious about her she would not go with him lest it delay his rush to safety. She promised to follow him at dawn. Dawn came and she did not arrive. On the gunboat Sun sat waiting, pretending to read, trying to be calm. Still she did not come.

What had happened was worse than he knew. Madame Sun could not leave the palace, for the rebel soldiers kept up a steady fire of guns and rifles over the building. At eight o'clock, however, most of their ammunition was gone. Then taking only the fewest necessities with her she crept out of the palace gates with two guards and a foreign adviser. Still under some fire but unseen, they moved from street to street to shelter in the government office in another part of the city. That place soon became unsafe and at four o'clock in the afternoon it was attacked. Madame Sun and her three companions escaped only by mingling with the attacking crowds. They were poorly dressed and were not recognized.

Where could they go? The city was on fire. Whole areas were raging furnaces, and as they hurried along a side street they saw a mob of half-crazed soldiers. They saved themselves only by lying down in the street and pretending to be dead. When the mob had passed, they crept on their way again. One of the guards was shot and killed, and Madame Sun was so exhausted that she begged the other guard to kill her, but he refused.

Slowly they reached the city gate, now un-guarded, and since they looked like refugees no one stopped them. Outside the city they took shelter in the house of a kindly farmer, and there Madame Sun rested. Two days later she was able to reach the water front and was taken to the ship where Sun Yat-sen had all but given her up. She arrived white and worn but alive, and the two lovers were together again.

That Canton battle, Sun Yat-sen said, was the worst experience of his whole life. All his books and manuscripts were burned, and he had to begin over again with his material as best he could remember it. Many more of his old friends were killed, and the city which he had tried to build into a beautiful and modern one was all but destroyed. Then, too, he felt deeply the betrayal of General Chen Chiung-ming. He had been fond of the able and bold young scholar-soldier, and whenever Sun was fond of a person he trusted him. More than once the person was not worthy either of love or trust.

Back in Shanghai once more Sun Yat-sen might have been tempted to give up forever. Instead he said, "We have destroyed too much. We must be rigorous, stern and unsentimental. It is time that we make a plan for the future and carry it out to the end. We must begin the great task of reconstruction or perish from the map of the world."

11

"Save My Country"

A PLAN! THIS MAN WAS ALWAYS PLANNING. HE
set himself to the task of rewriting his book. It
was still to be called *The Three Principles of the
People*, and in it he put down once more his ideas
for the future of the country.

While he was writing, the confusion in his
country went on. He could do nothing now to
stop it, except to grow angry at the foreign nations
who were using the war lords to get trade and

securities for their loans. Angry he was indeed at the greedy powers who fattened off the distress of the Chinese people! The only nations which did not try to benefit from China's confusion at that time, unfortunately for China's future, were the new Soviet Russia and the war-conquered Germany. Even the United States, with her open-door policy, was not willing to help Sun Yat-sen.

While China had been going through such hard times, Russia too had had a revolution—a terrible and cruel one. Many people had been killed and a harsh new government had been set up to compel the remaining people to develop their land collectively and build new industries. But Sun Yat-sen, always easily moved by anything like kindness, felt that Germany and Russia could help China more than the other Western powers who had made unequal treaties in her time of weakness. He had begun to correspond with the governments of both countries and he asked their advice.

His young general, Chiang Kai-shek, agreed with him.

Chiang said, "If countries like England, France, America and Japan are not anxious for the restoration of friendship and mutual assistance, why should not China conclude agreements with Germany and Russia?"

Thus, without meaning it, Sun Yat-sen nevertheless began a new confusion which was to end years later in the loss of the liberty of the Chinese people.

But of that future defeat mercifully Sun Yat-sen was never to know anything. One more fight he undertook against the war lords, although he did not know it was the last. Money was raised among his followers to train armies to punish the young rebel general, Chen Chiung-ming. In January, 1923, these armies converged upon Canton and the young general fled, disbanding his army as he went. Canton was regained, and became the southern capital once more. It could be used as a base for liberating the whole country from the war lords. Once again Sun Yat-sen returned to Canton as President. He appointed his son, now grown, to be the mayor, and the loyal soldier Chiang Kai-shek to be his chief of staff.

He had another enemy now, a secret one within himself. He was thin and tired and often he had terrible spasms of pain. Madame Sun was frightened when she saw the deathly pallor of his face, but he would not give up. No, first the whole country must be taken back from the warring war lords and united again, one indivisible Republic of China, under the five-barred flag. He set himself to build a new strong army under the direction of Chiang Kai-shek, for he had heard that Chen Chiung-ming was preparing to attack Canton yet again in the spring.

The attack came, and the battle lasted for two months in mud and rain. This time Sun Yat-sen commanded the soldiers himself. In an old hat and trench coat, he urged them on. He kept up their courage, refusing retreat. He knew something was very wrong with him now but he must not stop to find out what it was. Such spirit could not be defeated. He won, and Chen was driven away again.

Now, he said to his anxious, sad, young wife, now he would rebuild the revolutionary party. He would open a school in Canton where young men could be taught how to govern their country. They would be the nucleus, the heart of the new government. Last time he had entrusted the government to Yuan Shih-kai, a man who had not understood how to make a Republic. This time he would entrust it to young men whom he himself would train. He sent Chiang Kai-shek to Russia to learn how the Russians trained their young party members, and he invited to Canton a Russian adviser, Borodin. Years later Chiang Kai-shek

The battle lasted for two months in mud and rain

became alarmed at Borodin's power in a new outbreak of the Chinese Revolution and alarmed, too, at the influence he had over Madame Sun Yat-sen. Seeing these things, he determined to cut himself off from Borodin. So began Chiang's relentless war against Chinese Communists which might have been successful had it not been for a new war on China from Japan.

But of this, too, Sun Yat-sen was never to know. He continued to work to unify his country. Civil wars between the war lords broke out in a series of battles. Suddenly a strange thing happened. A huge young northern war lord, Feng Yu-hsiang, was unexpectedly successful in capturing Peking. He was unexpected in other ways, too. He turned out the other war lords, he banished the young Emperor from the summer palace, he set aside the weak President and he invited Sun Yat-sen to come to Peking and talk peace. In this miraculous way Sun saw the possibility of his dream coming true. North and South might be united with one great Republic, thanks to Feng Yu-hsiang.

He had paid no heed to his growing illness because he had so many other troubles, and now he was too happy to pay any heed to it. In November, 1924, he left Canton with his staff and of course his devoted wife. When he went, he told the people that now he hoped to make a real National

Assembly in the northern capital and he hoped to free the nation from the greed of foreign powers and help the people to a better life.

But the enemy within him was waiting. He went to Peking by way of Japan, and while he was in Japan he had to greet thousands of Chinese students and friends and make many speeches, too many for his strength. The sea between Japan and China is often stormy and cold and in winter always so. The voyage was rough and he caught influenza. He could not eat the ship's food and he had left his own cook in China and he felt very ill.

At the dock in Tientsin a tremendous crowd waited for him. Those who were near saw that his face was pale and that every now and again he gripped his right side as though he were in pain. But he held his head high, his eyes were proud, he wore a long black Chinese robe and he looked like a king. He spoke to the crowd, and then with Madame Sun he was taken in a car to the hotel.

People said he looked old but he was not old, only aged by all that he had been through and by the gnawing enemy within his body. Yet that night he had to go to a feast prepared for him by the war lord, Marshal Chang, who was in command of the province. Afterwards he spent three hours in conference. Then he went back to the hotel to bed.

He could not get up the next day or the next. Impatiently he worked in bed during the days to come and fretted because he could not go on to Peking. He sent his recommendations ahead and hoped that they would be accepted. Then he waited for two more weeks. By that time his influenza was well, but he still had the pain in his swollen liver. He was very restless until the reply came from the northern general in Peking with whom he had hoped to make peace. It brought bad news. All his recommendations were rejected, and worse than this, General Feng had promised the foreign nations that their special rights would not be disturbed.

At this Sun Yat-sen sprang from his bed in a fury. "I am determined to abolish all the unequal treaties!" he shouted. "Why did you invite me to the North? Do you fear these foreigners?"

His doctors made him go to bed again, but he was determined to get to Peking. Ten days later in a special car he reached the city. He was too weak to speak more than a few words and he went to bed at once in a hotel room. Yet not for a moment did he give up his dream of uniting the North and South into one nation, here and now. His mind was not always clear as he lay there in his bed, and those who were with him, his beautiful young wife always at his side, heard him murmuring under his breath, planning, planning. But he could not move. For ten days he lay in his bed, and then he was taken to the great Peking Hospital, which had been built by Americans. There an American surgeon operated on him. When he opened the thin and agonized body, he found the liver as hard as stone with cancer. Nothing could be done. It was too late. He sewed up the wound and though violet rays were used in a last hope, they did no good.

In February, when the first touch of spring comes to the city of Peking, when the golden buds of the leafless lamay trees begin to swell and the dusty winds to blow from the Gobi deserts, Sun Yat-sen was taken to the home of a friend to die. Chinese doctors were called in to see if they could do what the foreign doctors could not, but they, too, were helpless. Sun Yat-sen knew that he must die with his dream unfulfilled. At night he wept bitterly, but in the daytime he lay quiet and still.

On February the twenty-fourth, in the afternoon, the last hours seemed near. His beloved wife, his son and his grandson and a few friends were in the room. Could he speak to them? They longed to hear his final commands, his advice, for what would they do without him? One of his most faithful men, Wang Ching-wei, came to the bedside and asked him if he could speak to them.

"If I must die," Sun Yat-sen said, "it is useless to say anything."

They begged him to speak to them a few last words.

"I see that you are in real danger," he whispered at last. "When I am dead, our enemies will weaken you—or destroy you. What can I say now?"

"We have followed you for many years," Wang Ching-wei urged. "We have not been afraid, nor have we been weakened by the enemy. If you leave us a message, it will guide us."

"What do you want me to say?" Sun Yat-sen asked.

"We have written down what we think you would like to say to us," Wang replied. "If you agree please sign it—although we could wish you would speak your own words."

Wang Ching-wei read the statement which had been prepared and Sun Yat-sen nodded his head. "Very well," he said, "I do agree."

A second document was then read, a brief will, leaving his few possessions to his beloved wife. He nodded his head again.

He was about to make the effort to sign these two documents when he turned his head and saw his wife leaning against the door, weeping bitterly. He was overcome with his own grief then and could not sign, and the documents were taken away.

But he signed them a few days later when he himself knew the end was near. He had received a telegram telling him that the war in the South was almost over and that General Chiang Kai-shek had matters well in hand. He sent his reply, a final telegram, saying that "the citizens of Canton must not be disturbed by our military forces." His thought was always for his people. On that afternoon of March the eleventh he was breathing with great difficulty. In the evening he called for the two documents and with the help of his wife, who lifted his hand, he signed his name to them.

Then when he had rested a few minutes he spoke these words in a faint and broken voice.

"I thought I would come here to set up our national unity and peace. I planned to have a People's Convention and put into practice my *Three Principles of the People* and the Five-Power Constitution for the building of a new China. Instead I have been seized by a stupid disease and now I am past all cure. To live or to die makes no difference to me personally but not to achieve all that I have struggled for through so many years grieves me to the heart. You who live, strive for the People's Convention, try to put into practice the Three Principles, and the Constitution. Then I can rest."

He paused and after a while he said, "I have tried to be a messenger of God—to help my people to get equality—and freedom."

They were all listening for his last words. In

"PEACE—STRUGGLE, SAVE MY COUNTRY!"

Sun Yat-sen, the man who changed China

China the last words of a good man are precious. They are carved upon wood and written into the family records. But the foreign doctor begged Sun Yat-sen to rest. He fell asleep for a while and when he woke in the early evening his hands and feet were cold. Yet he lived through the night, still clinging to his dream. They heard him murmuring a few words, "Peace——struggle——save my country——"

The next morning he died. His wife was with him, and upon her his last look rested.

So lived and died a great man. Though Sun Yat-sen did not see the unified China he had tried to build, he changed forever that mighty country to which he belonged with all his heart. Had he lived could he have fulfilled the dream? Who knows? Perhaps it was not necessary for him to live. Perhaps the dream must be fulfilled by the people themselves.

Today the people of China live under a great shadow. A free and unified China seems further away than ever. But the dream still lives in Chinese hearts. Sun Yat-sen planted it there, deep and true. Whatever the present bondage, they cannot forget. They cannot forget for they do not forget Sun Yat-sen. The body of that brave and selfless man lies in a marble tomb on the sunny side of Purple Mountain outside the walls of Nanking. But he lives on. He lives in the minds and hearts of millions of Chinese. Some day his soul will march again, in them, and they will win their country for their own at last.

Index

Agriculture, 34
Americans, 118
Ancestors, 17
Annam, Indo-China, 101, 103, 105, 106
Anti-Manchu secret societies, 29
Army, 74, 78

Bankers, 143
Bishop's School. *See* Iolani
Borodin (adviser), 170
Boxer Rebellion, 78-81, 85, 96
British Maritime Customs, 45

Calendar, 124
California, 12-13
Cantile, Sir James, 30-32, 46, 51-52, 54-56, 59-63, 119-120
Canton, China, 7, 28, 46, 49, 65, 81, 97-98, 106, 128, 134, 159, 160, 164, 167-69, 171, 177
Chang Chih-tung, 68, 173
Charge to Learn, A, 68
Chen Chiung-ming (general), 160, 164, 167-69
Cheng Shih-liang, 28-30, 74, 81-82
Chiang Kai-shek, 160, 167-70, 177
China: army, 74, 78; civilization, 2; conquerors, 74; defence forces, 28-29; democracy, 76, 88-89; elder brother, 25; government, *see* Government; hundred years ago, 1-6, 12-13; Japan and, *see* Japan; navy, 74, 78; patriotism, 135; patriots, 43; people, 85, 126, 157; railroads, 72, 120, 137-38; revolution, 97-98, 100, 102, 104, 106; secret societies, 74-75; 81, 90, 97-99; spheres of influence, 67; unified, 180-81
Chinatowns, 90-93, 108
Chinese Legation, London, 59, 62, 63

Chinese Patriotic Society, 92
Choyhung (village), 6
Christian missionary schools, 76-77
Christianity, 17-18, 24-25, 26, 30, 58-59, 77, 90
Civil Wars, 128, 130, 142-64, 171
Classics, The, 10
Clemenceau, 121
Communists, 170
Confucius, 41
Consortium, 120, 138-40
Constitution, 127, 156

Dare-to-Dies, 103
Democracy, 76, 88-89
Denver, Colorado, 113
Dowager Empress. *See* Empress Dowager
Dreams, 145

Education (public), 34, 86, 155
Emperor, 67-69, 84, 112
Empress, 129, 137
Empress Dowager, The, 68, 69, 71, 73, 78, 80, 85-86, 112
England, 5, 51, 67, 69-70, 118-20, 167
English (language), 16, 19, 23
Europe, 69-70, 93

Feet binding, 13
Feng Yu-hsiang (war lord), 171, 173-74
Flag, 132, 168
Foochow (city), 29
Formosa, 45, 81-82
France, 28-29, 67, 72-73, 101-04, 118, 167
French Revolution, 125-27
Fukien (province), 29

Germany, 67, 72, 118, 166-67
Globe, The (newspaper), 62
Government, 20, 21, 26, 39, 41, 45, 54, 70, 72, 78, 81, 84, 88-89, 99,

116–18, 126–28, 130. 138–40, 145, 151, 157–58

Hager, Charles, 24, 26
Hainan (island), 65
Hankow, 73, 113
Hawaii, 13, 14, 16, 48–49
Hongkong, 16, 23, 26, 30, 46, 48, 44, 81, 121–22
Honolulu 36–38, 43, 70, 89
Hsing Chung Huei, or Prosper China Society, 38, 90
Hsu Shih-chang, 42
Hu Han-min, 122
Huang Hsing, 103, 105, 140
Hunan, 68
Hupeh, 68

I Hsing, 92
Indo-China, 29
Inukai, 70–71
Iolani (school), 14, 16, 19

Japan, 35–36, 39, 44–45, 48, 67, 70–71, 73, 81–82, 83, 85, 87, 89, 101, 103, 104, 105, 118–19, 142, 167, 172
Jones, Charles, 43–44

Kang Yu-wei, 69, 87–90, 97, 112
Kemingtang, 152
Kerr, Dr. John, 26–28
Kiangsi Province, 114
Kiukiang (city), 140
Korea, 45
Kung, H. H., 147
Kuomintang, 139, 152
Kwangchow-wan, 67

Lea, Homer, 94, 95–97, 108–09, 113, 121, 128
Li Hung-chang (Viceroy), 33–34, 36, 42
Li Kung, 41–42
Li Yuan-hung, 154–55, 159
Liang Chi-chao, 69, 112, 154
Linebarger, Judge, 100

Literati, 72
Liu Hao-tung, 20, 21, 23, 28, 33, 46
Lives and Work of the Ching Scholars, The, 42
London, England, 54–55, 69, 119

Macao, 31–32, 46
Macartney, Sir Halliday, 55–56, 63
Manila, 100–01
Manchu government, 4, 10, 29, 43, 48–49, 52, 60, 75, 99, 101, 103, 104, 111, 118, 120, 124–25, 128, 158
Manchuria, 67, 72
Manson, Sir Patrick, 60
Mings (dynasty), 75, 123, 133–34
Mission schools, 76–77
Monarchy, 42–43, 87

Nakagama, Mr., 84
Nanking, 123
Nanking Council, 130
National Assembly, 122
Navy, 74, 78
New York, 119

Obedience, 25
Okuma, 70–71
Old Bailey Court, 62
Opium, 5

Pao Huang Huei or Save the Emperor Society, 87–89
Pearl River Delta, 46
Peking, China, 67, 73, 80, 85, 136–38, 171
Peoples' Paper, The (newspaper), 101
Policemen, 157
Port Arthur, 67
President of China, 116–17, 120, 122, 130, 149, 154–55, 159, 168
Prosper China Society, 38, 90
Provinces, 138
Purple Mountain, 123, 181

Queens College, Hongkong, 23
Queue, 48

Index

Railroads, 72, 120, 137–38
Reform Cadets, 96–97
Reformers, 87
"Republican Form of Government" (speech), 155
Revolution, 39–40, 46, 51, 53, 73, 144
Revolution (First), 96
Revolution (Second), 152–53
Revolution (Third), 154
Rice, price of, 5
Roosevelt, Theodore, 94
Russia, 72, 118
Russia (Soviet), 166–67, 169, 170
Russo-Japanese War, 89

Salisbury, Lord, 63
San Francisco, California, 52–53, 96
Scholars, 72–73, 75, 76
Science, 17, 20
Scotland Yard, 60–62
Secret societies, 74–75, 81, 90, 97–99
Shanghai, 122, 159
Shantung, 72
Si-an (city), 80
Siberia, 72
Singapore, 105–06, 121
Soong, Charles, 43–44, 146–47
Soong Ai-lien, 147
Soong Ching-ling, 148, 150, 151
Southern Republic, 156
Sun Ah-mei, 6, 13, 14, 16, 17, 25, 48–50, 146, 149
Sun Annie, 150
Sun family, 6–9, 22–24, 149
Sun Fo (son), 32, 150, 159
Sun Yat-sen: America, 12–13; childhood, 7–9; death, 175–80; dedication, 49; education, 9–14, 16–18, 22–26, 30; exile, 141; failures, 110; honesty, 38; influenza, 172–73; illness, 171; integrity, 67; marked man, 64–66; marriage

(first), 24; oratory, 37; organizer, 144; pain, 168–69; parents, 146, 149; popularity, 135; price upon his head, 64; prisoner, 56–57; revolutionist, 39–50; tomb, 181; wife, 146, 148–49, 151
Sun Yat-sen, Mme., 148, 150, 151, 162–63, 168–72, 174–80
Sung Chiao-jen, 139–40

Taiping Rebellion, 4–5
Taxation, 5, 99, 103
Three-Character Classic, The, 10
Three Principles of the People, The, 101, 158–59, 165, 178
Tientsin, 33, 172
Tokyo, Japan, 71
Tongking, 29
"Tongs," 90–92
Treaties, 174
Triad, The (society), 30
Tsingtao (port), 67
Tuan Chi-jui (Premier), 155

United States, 51–52, 108, 166–67

Valor of Ignorance, The, 97

Wang, Dr. C. T., 156
Wang Ching-wei, 176–77
War lords, 155–56, 159, 165, 167, 171
Weihaiwei, 67
Western books, 42
Woosung, 102
World War (First), 150, 151, 155, 159
Wu Pei-fu, 159
Wuchang (city), 102, 114

Yen Yuan, 41
Yokohama, Japan, 83
Yuan Shih-kai, 34, 42, 43, 68–69, 125, 128–34, 136–41, 143–46, 151, 152, 153, 154, 157–58, 169
Yunnan, 29, 105, 154